Praise for
Finding Joy in the Morning

I love the straightforward simplistic nature of this book. It is an easy read, yet deeply profound at the same time. I love the 'stop and pray with me' sections and the questions at the end of the chapters. It's a wonderful book that will help many people to understand who they really are in God's eyes and how they can have a deeper and more meaningful relationship with Him.

Sandi Vidal, Executive Director, Christian HELP

Finding Joy in the Morning guides readers through troubling times using faith-based suggestions, such as believing and obeying, seeing problems as gifts, living in the moment, and practicing forgiveness. The author includes related quotes, prayers, and "Your Turn" ideas, which are interactive questions for readers to apply these concepts to their own lives. The writing is clear, crisp, friendly, and professional, making this work the perfect follow-up to Jacquelyn Lynn's earlier book, *Words to Work By: 31 devotions for the workplace based on the Book of Proverbs*.

Leslie C. Halpern, Author
200 *Love Lessons from the Movies* and *Passionate About Their Work*

Finding Joy in the Morning spoke to my heart about concerns that affect me every day. It was encouraging, not preachy. It was easy to read, like having a conversation with a close friend. I'll read this book again and again, and gain something new each time. I loved it. I wish everyone in my church could read it!

Kim Rooks

This is a book for anybody to read, but especially those who label themselves Christians. Those of us who are trying to grow in our faith will be encouraged and gain workable ideas about keeping that faith alive and thriving. Those who just attend church and think that is sufficient should be inspired to put into action one or two of Jacquelyn's many suggestions.
Ruth Ford

As I began reading *Finding Joy in the Morning* I felt relaxed, clear-headed and happy. This book was guiding me to understand how I can be closer to God and be able to solve many more issues in my life.
Susan Boylston Adams

I really enjoyed reading *Finding Joy in the Morning*, it was an easy read, very thought provoking, uplifting and inspirational. I would highly recommend it to both my Christian and non-Christian friends.
Susan Harrison

Finding Joy in the Morning is a very practical and applicable book for everyday life. It would be excellent for a small study group.
Barbara Kulick

Love Jacquelyn's writing!! She has a gift of words that soothe the soul and which can leave one feeling refreshed and encouraged.
Amazon Reviewer

Everyone has rough and tough times. *Finding Joy in the Morning* is a very helpful book for dealing with those difficult times. It is well written and filled with the grace and love of God. The book is an excellent guide to getting in touch with God and staying close to God when you probably need Him most. After reading the book, I gave copies to two of my relatives who have recently lost a close family member.
Amazon Reviewer

Finding Joy
in the
Morning

You *can* make it through the night

Second Edition
Expanded & Updated

Jacquelyn Lynn

Copyright © 2017 by Jacquelyn Lynn.

Cover design: Jerry D. Clement
Interior design & production: Tuscawilla Creative Services

All rights reserved. No part of this publication may be reproduced, distributed or transmitted in any form or by any means, including photocopying, recording, or other electronic or mechanical methods, without the prior written permission of the publisher, except in the case of brief quotations embodied in critical reviews and certain other noncommercial uses permitted by copyright law. Send permission requests to Permissions Coordinator at info@contacttcs.com.

TCS

Tuscawilla Creative Services
www.CreateTeachInspire.com

For bulk orders, contact info@contacttcs.com.

Finding Joy in the Morning: You can make it through the night / Jacquelyn Lynn — 2nd ed.

ISBN 978-1-941826-20-1

The cover image by Jerry D. Clement depicts the joy and promise that each new sunrise brings. The lighthouse beacon symbolizes God who guides us from dark, storm-tossed seas to the safe harbor of home.

*Weeping may endure for a night,
but joy comes in the morning.*

Psalm 30:5 (AKJV)

CONTENTS

Introduction to the Second Edition	xi
Part I: Getting Through the Night	**1**
1 The Backstory	5
2 Know Who You Are	13
3 Have Faith in God	35
4 Live in the Moment	49
5 Understand the Importance of Community	67
6 Practice Forgiveness	81
7 Stay On Track (Close to God)	91
8 Problems are Gifts	111
9 Let God Be In Control and Watch What Happens	121
Part II: How to Find Joy Every Day	**125**
Index to Part II	177

Introduction to the Second Edition

The second edition of *Finding Joy in the Morning* didn't start out as a second edition.

It started out as a separate follow-up book to *Finding Joy* with the working title *Have a Joyful Day*. After more time than it should have taken, I finally finished the first draft and was starting to think about the cover and interior design. As I prayed for guidance and inspiration, God told me that *Joyful Day* was not a separate book, that it was part of *Finding Joy*. Along with that message came the answers to a list of production, marketing, and distribution questions.

Part I of the second edition is the original *Finding Joy in the Morning* with some updates. It shares the techniques that will help you get through life's greatest challenges. Part II includes more than 40 things you can do every day to make your life joyful.

We are meant to have joy in our lives. God calls us to rejoice and be joyful always. This doesn't mean we won't face trials—we absolutely will. This doesn't mean we won't experience pain, betrayal, and tragedy—those things are part of life. But when we learn to find joy in and through everything we do, we are living the life God wants for us. And that, my friend, is pure joy of the highest kind.

Jacquelyn Lynn

Part I

Getting Through the Night

As you read ...

At the end of each chapter in Part I, you'll find a prayer followed by questions under the heading "Your Turn." Please use these questions for private introspection or for discussion in a group study.

Chapter 1

The Backstory

Several years ago I was working on a project with a client who wanted me to ghostwrite his autobiography. He had faced and overcome some tremendous challenges and he wanted to share his story.

Before we could finish his book, some new obstacles appeared in his life and he abandoned the project.

In the process of trying to help him organize his thoughts and articulate his message, I learned some valuable lessons. As he talked about his life, I thought about my own experiences and about others I know who have shown amazing strength and resilience in the face of seemingly insurmountable challenges. I thought about the people who somehow manage to enjoy incredible peace during some of life's toughest times. I thought about how they did it. And I realized how much they had in common.

To be very clear here at the beginning: This is not a self-help book. While what I'm going to share with you is definitely going to improve your life, this is not a book that will teach you how to do it yourself. I couldn't do it alone, none of the people I've learned from could do it alone, and you can't do it alone, either.

Millions have felt inspired by William Ernest Henley's famous poem, "Invictus," which closes with these two lines: "I am the master of my fate; I am the captain of my soul." Any inspiration you might feel from those lines is temporary because they're simply not true.

> "God cannot give us a happiness and peace apart from Himself, because it is not there. There is no such thing."
> C. S. Lewis

It's human nature to want to be in control—but we are not. We are powerless, we are helpless, we are totally dependent on God. Life is not something we are made to handle alone; we need God and each other. We are made to be part of God's family, part of the body of Christ. If we try to do it on our own, we will fail—and we will be miserable.

Paul explains this very clearly in his first

letter to the Corinthians. He writes, "Now the body is not made up of one part but of many." (1 Corinthians 12:14) After he explains how the parts of the body work together for the whole, he says, "If one part suffers, every part suffers with it; if one part is honored, every part rejoices with it." (1 Corinthians 12:26)

When you understand that, accept it, and live it, it won't matter how out-of-control the world gets because you know God is in control and you'll be at peace.

With that understanding, let's explore how God gets us through the night to find joy in the morning.

Please Pray With Me

Father,

We come to you in praise for being the awesome God that you are. Your amazing power is beyond our human understanding. We know you are with us always, and we surrender ourselves to you.

We thank you for your goodness, for your greatness. Because we know that we are powerless on our own, we ask that you be with us and guide us as we seek to live the life you have planned for us.

We pray in the name of your Son and our Lord, Jesus Christ.

Amen

Your Turn

Who are the people in your life who support and sustain you? Think about what they mean to you. Have you shared that with them, either by telling them in person or writing to them? How did they respond?

_____
_____
_____

Have you ever been in a crisis situation and been helped by a total stranger? How did it make you feel?

_____
_____
_____

Think about ways to maintain your relationship with God when you are not in crisis. How can you apply those techniques to your life?

_____
_____
_____

Chapter 2

Know Who You Are

Who are you?

You are a child of God.

This very simple statement is, for many of us, an extremely difficult concept to grasp. But once you understand and accept it, once you know deep within yourself that you have a Heavenly Father who loves you mightily and wonderfully, you will live a life of fullness and peace, no matter what your circumstances.

Nothing else in our human experience compares to the love of a parent for a child. Creating another human being establishes a powerful bond, a love that is so deep and strong it must be experienced to be understood and believed. Yet as awesome as this parent/child love is, God's love for us is so much more because it's not restricted by our human limitations. Being a child of God means being loved unconditionally by a parent who is truly all-powerful. Earthly parents, in their humanity, are not perfect, but God is. God never gets tired, or grouchy, or loses his temper. To paraphrase the line made famous in the 1970 movie *Love Story*, God never has to say he's sorry.

Of course, God is not our biological father; he is more like an adoptive father. We can put this in human terms by thinking of someone who chooses to adopt a child and loves that child with the same, or even greater, depth and breadth than a biological parent does. God chose us to be his children. As strong as any parent's love is, consider how much stronger is the love of God for us, his adopted children.

A pastor once told me that she's careful not to spend too much time referring to God as "Father" when she's preaching or speaking to groups because so many people have issues with their earthly fathers and therefore have a hard time with the concept of a loving Heavenly Father. I understand and appreciate that, but I look at it from a different perspective. I don't have a great relationship with my biological father. He and my mother divorced when I was young and he did not play a significant role in my life after that. He was not abusive and he honored his financial obligations, but he just wasn't there in any meaningful way—something even he acknowledges now. So I see God as an awesome father, the one I didn't have as a child. Rather than having an issue with God as *a* father, I am grateful for God *the* Father.

As a father, God is always there, always supporting you, sometimes with tough love, sometimes with gentle love. He's not an enabler; he won't stop you from making a mistake if you're determined to do so. But he's always there to wisely guide you out of whatever mess you've made for yourself and comfort you when you're hurting.

We are all children of God because he is our Creator. Even more, he is the Creator of the universe and everything in it. When we talk about being a child of God in the Biblical sense, we are talking about our belief and trust in him.

> Then, because you belong to Christ Jesus, God will bless you with peace that no one can completely understand. And this peace will control the way you think and feel.
> *Philippians 4:7 (CEV)*

Many of us have the wrong idea of how God feels about us. We may think we can never measure up to what God expects or that God gets angry with us because we are not perfect and we can't seem to stop sinning, even when we know better. We may even think that God doesn't care about us because he lets bad things happen to us. None of that is true.

To God, you are a beloved child, and God's love for his children never wavers. To know the joy of that love, all you need to do is accept it.

Who Are You?

We tend to define ourselves by things that aren't really important—our occupation, our hobbies, even our relatives. Or we define ourselves by what has happened to us or things we've done. These things may be descriptions of our lives, but they are not who we are.

Try this experiment: The next time you're in a small group, ask everyone to describe who they are in ten words or less without saying their name. Depending on the nature of the group, you're likely to hear things like:

"I am a police officer."
"I am a baseball card collector."
"I am George's wife."
"I am a teacher."
"I am Sean's brother."
"I am an actor."
"I am Ashley's mother."
"I am a golfer."

What you may not hear, but what these people are likely saying to themselves, are things like:

"I am a failure."
"I am a cheater."
"I am a loser."

While the things that are said out loud are all probably true, and the things that are thought but not spoken may or may not be true, what you really are, first and foremost, is a child of God.

Try saying it now, out loud: "I am a child of God."

If it feels a little awkward, that's understandable. Keep on saying it until it feels comfortable—until you believe it. Keep saying it until it's the first thing you think of whenever you think about who you are. Accept that, before you are anything else, you are a child of God, destined for a life wrapped in the security provided by your Heavenly Father.

> The Lord also says, "Then I will welcome you and be your Father. You will be my sons and my daughters, as surely as I am God, the All-Powerful."
>
> 2 Corinthians 6:17-18 (CEV)

A Label You Can Love

We live in a culture that loves labels. We slap them on everything. The problem is that once we're labeled, we have a hard time escaping from that identification and discovering our true selves. We see this everywhere in our society, from children who get labeled as "special needs" (which apparently means anything from a mild learning disorder to a major mental illness) to public figures who are identified with something that is a very small part of their lives, and even to the everyday people with whom we work, attend school, and socialize.

FINDING JOY IN THE MORNING

Such labeling gets in the way of who we really are: a child of God—and that's a label you can welcome, appreciate, and love.

There's a great story about the late Ben Hooper, who was governor of Tennessee from 1911 to 1915. Hooper's mother was not married, and there was a substantial amount of stigma attached to illegitimate children back then. According to the story, Hooper was in his early teens when a preacher spoke to him after church one Sunday. The preacher asked, "Who are you, son? Whose boy are you?" Before Hooper could answer, the preacher said, "Wait a minute. I know who you are. I see the family resemblance. You are a son of God. Boy, you've got a great inheritance. Go and claim it."

> "God didn't make a mistake when He made you. You need to see yourself as God sees you."
>
> Joel Osteen

While there is some disagreement over whether that meeting actually happened and, if so, exactly what the preacher said, the message is worth remembering. Hooper, born in 1870, was illegitimate, spent part of his childhood in an orphanage, worked as a church janitor in his youth, and yet still became a lawyer and was eventually elected governor of Tennessee. Hooper knew he didn't have to be bound by human labels; he knew that God had a plan for him. This is what it means to be a child of

God, a child with an awesome inheritance just waiting to be claimed.

A Wonderful Difference

We are created in God's image. Just as human children resemble their parents, we resemble God. I think that's at least partly why so many of us are control freaks—God has the ability to control absolutely everything in existence, and we'd like to be able to do the same. But just as human children are not exact duplicates of their parents, we are not precise copies of God. If we were, we would be all-powerful and perfect. We're not.

All of God's children are different. We all have unique spiritual gifts. We all have our own special purpose. There is no one else in the world exactly like you, and there never will be. When God made you, he broke the mold.

This is part of God's plan. It's God's way of letting each of us know how special we are to him, how much we matter to him.

Why Does God Let Bad Things Happen to His Children?

Let's begin this discussion by admitting that "bad" is a subjective word. What is bad to me may not be bad to you. Bad is also a matter of perspective. What is a tragedy to me may be a mere inconvenience to you.

Regardless of our perception, the fact is

that bad things happen. Innocent people who just happen to be in the wrong place at the wrong time get hit by cars and assaulted by criminals. Weather events (tornados, earthquakes, hurricanes, thunderstorms) injure and kill people and destroy property. Planes crash, trains derail, ships sink. I could go on with this list, but I won't. I don't have an answer nor do I understand why things like this happen, but I do have peace with the fact that they do.

We don't need all the answers in life to experience peace. Peace comes from knowing that God has all the answers and that someday you will, too. In the meantime, find rest in surrendering your questions to God, trusting that he may or may not provide the answers. He may or may not deliver you from the storm, but he will be with you in the midst of it and he will bring you through it.

It's crucial that we clarify one important thing: God does not cause bad things to happen. What happens to us and to the people we love is not always fair. It doesn't always make sense. But God is not hateful. He is not cruel. God has given his children free will, which means we can choose to do bad things. Because we are connected and not designed to go through this time on Earth alone, the bad things we choose to do can affect others—and they usually do.

Know this: God does not wish harm on any of his children. It is never God's will that we experience pain and suffering. When we are hurt, he feels our pain every bit as deeply, if not more, than we do, which is why he provides comfort and strength for us when we are in times of trial. Just as human parents wisely turn challenging times into teaching moments ("Billy, you fell down and skinned your knee because you weren't looking where you were going. I'm going to kiss your knee and make it better, but I want you to remember this: When you pay attention, you won't trip and fall."), God does the same.

God gave us free will, and that includes being able to make choices. Some of those choices are simple and insignificant (chocolate or vanilla); some are complex and major (good or evil). God won't stop us from choosing evil if that's what we decide to do. The reason is simple: If we aren't free to choose evil, then we aren't free to choose good. If we cannot choose good for ourselves, our choices are not authentic.

> Think how much the Father loves us. He loves us so much that he lets us be called his children, as we truly are.
>
> 1 John 3:1 (CEV)

When we choose evil, bad things happen. Maybe not immediately, and often not only to the person who made the choice, but without a doubt, bad things happen. That's one of the things many people have a hard time with—that even when people are doing their best, making good choices, not hurting others, something bad could still happen to them.

That reality makes it easy to question God. That's okay because God knows the answers. What he wants you to focus on is that he always brings good out of the bad—always! He has a wonderful way of bringing out the best in us when circumstances are at their worst.

Remember that God can see the whole picture—past, present, and future—of all creation, everywhere. And he weaves it all together in a way our human minds can't fully comprehend. But we can understand it enough to know that we are all connected even when it isn't readily apparent.

> "I think of life as a good book. The further you get into it, the more it begins to make sense."
>
> Harold S. Kushner

Here's how God has used bad things for good results in my life: I'd been thinking about writing this book for a long time, but was just "too busy," primarily with things I was doing for my church. Then I did Beth Moore's *Breaking Free* study and realized that all of the church "stuff" I was doing was not only just "stuff," it was a form of bondage that was interfering with my relationship with God and preventing me from living out his purpose for my life.

When I made the decision to shed many of the church responsibilities I had accumulated over the years, I knew immediately from the peace I felt that God had spoken to me through Beth Moore's study and I had heard him accurately. However, the actual process of breaking free from the bondage of all that church work that had nothing to do with worship was not easy. And there were times that I was tempted to pick up some of the tasks I'd put down. But things happened to stop me—things that, from the outside, looked bad: Both my father and my aunt (who served as a surrogate mother to me since my own mother died years ago) suffered some serious health-related issues, and I spent a lot of time providing them with support and care. They took priority and I simply didn't have enough hours in the day to do what I needed to do with and for them and do church work as well.

Now, did God cause my relatives' health problems solely to keep me on track? I don't think so. But did he use them to bring me closer to him and move me in the direction he wants me to go? Yes, without question. I began working on this project in earnest while sitting in my aunt's hospital room as she slept. And having to take my father for two outpatient surgeries and follow-up visits kept me from sliding back into doing church tasks I'd said I wasn't going to do anymore. By the way, those tasks got done by others—not exactly the way I did them, but they were done, I was at peace and now you're reading this book. Taking it all to still another level: My father suffered some rare complications during what should have been routine cataract surgery. Those complications required a second procedure by a different surgeon to correct. The first surgeon told us that he learned some things from the complications my father experienced that would change the way he operated in the future, and that change in technique would reduce the chances something similar would happen to someone else. Though my aunt died shortly after the first edition of this book was published, my father fully recovered and, as I write this, is doing well.

Can God stop bad things from happening if he wants to—even the bad things from someone's deliberate choice? I believe he can and often does. I have no idea how many bad things he has chosen to prevent in my life—I'm sure I can't count that high. Did he stop every bad thing? No. Was he there for me as I worked through the consequences of my decisions and actions? Absolutely—even when I was pushing him away.

Don't *blame* God when bad things happen. Instead, *trust* him to get you through whatever situation you're in and to bless you in the process.

What Does God Want for You?

God wants more for you than you could ever know—and the most important thing he wants for you is that you fulfill the purpose he had in mind when he created you. It is so easy to fall into the trap of thinking that we are just one of many, that we're not unique, and that we don't really matter. Nothing could be further from the truth.

You've probably heard the phrase, "God doesn't make junk." That's true. It's also true that God doesn't do anything by accident. There is nothing random about his creation. God made everything—including you—for a purpose. Just as you need God, God needs you. When you understand and fulfill God's purpose for your life, you will know a joy words cannot describe.

> "God asks no man whether he will accept life. That is not the choice. One must take it. The only choice is how."
>
> Henry Ward Beecher

How do you find out what God's purpose for your life is?

Just ask him.

Yes, it really is that simple—but it's not necessarily easy. The challenge comes in hearing God amid the information clutter that dominates so much of our lives and in knowing for sure that it's God speaking to you.

I wish I could tell you that all it takes to hear God clearly is to go to a quiet place and pray. I know that's one way to do it, but it's not the only way. We'll be talking more about prayer and about staying close to God in Chapter Seven, but for now, the challenge we want to address is how to know you are truly hearing God.

When you ask God questions—whether you're asking about what your purpose is or something else—here's how to verify the answer:

Be sure it conforms to Scripture. God is consistent and he won't tell us to do anything that doesn't conform to his Word. Whatever God's purpose for you is, you can be absolutely certain that it will be loving, honest, and kind.

Look for signs of confirmation. Those signs may come from circumstances, they may come from other people, or they may come from your own feelings of peace and confidence.

Consider the big picture. Look at your life over a long period of time to see if the message you're hearing fits with how God has been working with you. God doesn't just assign a purpose and surprise us with it, he equips us to fulfill it.

Ask for clarification. If you're not sure what you're being told, feel free to say, "God, I'm not sure I understood. Please tell me what you mean." He'll make it clear.

> "When the solution is simple, God is answering."
>
> Albert Einstein

As you are trying to learn your purpose, be patient. Remember that God's time is not our time. He may not reveal everything to you when you ask because you may not be ready to know it. And what seems like a purpose right now may actually be preparation for something more later. Just always know that if you talk to God regularly, you'll know that he's guiding you in his plan.

So ask God what he wants for you—and be prepared for the answer to be something you didn't expect.

What It Means to be a Child of God

Being a child of God makes you one of God's heirs. God has given each of his children an inheritance of incalculable value. This means that you are going to receive all the goodness that God gives. No matter how loved and secure you might feel, you are actually more loved and more secure than you know. You belong to him, you are part of his family, and you can never lose that identity.

> This is what the Lord says: "Cursed is the one who trusts in man, who depends on flesh for his strength and whose heart turns away from the Lord. ... But blessed is the man who trusts in the Lord, whose confidence is in him."
> *Jeremiah 17:5, 7 (NIV)*

Does this mean you're going to win the Powerball lottery next week? Probably not. That's not what it's all about. Although God wants his children to enjoy the material world, he does not give us everything we ask for. Yes, sometimes he gives us what we want for no other reason than to make us happy. Other times, instead of simply giving us what we think we want (such as an unearned cash windfall), he blesses us with gifts that will allow us to obtain what we want and are willing to work for. Always, in his wisdom, God goes beyond what we want and gives us what we need. At the same time, he guides and disciplines us so we can mature into the people he wants us to be.

God wants us to relate to him as a child to a parent because he wants us to recognize that he and he alone knows what's best for us.

Something else about being one of God's children is this: God wants us to love him. He wants us to do it voluntarily, using the free will he has given us.

We know that in our human relationships, we cannot make someone love us, no matter how much we wish we could. Love can't be forced. There is no gift greater than love freely given without any sort of coercion or conditions. That's the love God gives to us, and it's the love he wants in return.

> "What surprises me most about God is that the creator of the universe should want a relationship with me."
>
> Rick Warren

Love your Heavenly Father—not because you have to, but because you choose to.

Just as God doesn't force us to love him, he doesn't force us to do anything else. He has given us free will, which means we can decide whether to obey him or not, whether to live his purpose for us or not. In addition to being free to choose good, being a child of God also means that we are forgiven when we don't. We'll talk more about forgiveness later in Chapter Six, but the important point here is that God has forgiven our sins—past, present, and future. He sent His son Jesus Christ to die on the cross so our sins would be washed away. It's that simple and that complicated.

> "I'm not perfect. I'm never going to be. And that's the great thing about living the Christian life and trying to live by faith, is you're trying to get better every day. You're trying to improve."
>
> *Tim Tebow*

God knows we are sinners. He forgives us, even knowing that we are likely to sin again—and when we do, he forgives again. However, we shouldn't take this as a license to do what we want, when we want, without any regard for right or wrong.

I remember when I was a kid thinking that Catholics had it pretty good because they could do what they wanted even if it was wrong, go to confession, chant some prayers for penance then do what they wanted again. That's a superficial perspective and not the right idea behind confessing our sins and asking for forgiveness.

FINDING JOY IN THE MORNING

God forgives our sins when we are truly sorry and ask for his help and guidance to move past the sin. But if we're continually sinning and think, "Oh, I don't have to worry, God will forgive me," we're wrong. A sin committed once or twice is a mistake; done repeatedly, it becomes a choice. There comes a point when God holds you accountable for your actions. But when we go to him in true repentance, no matter how horrific the sin, we will be forgiven.

The concept that God will forgive the worst of sins is difficult for many people to fully grasp. You may think you've drifted so far away from God or done things that are so bad that God will never take you back and forgive you. That is absolutely not true. If you sincerely confess your sins to God and ask for his forgiveness, you will have it. This is what it means to be a child of God.

As God's children, we can expect and rely on a Heavenly Father who is loving, gracious, tender, and compassionate. We can be secure in our knowledge that God will take care of us. And we can be simple and child-like in our love for Him.

Please Pray With Me

Heavenly Father,

Help us to know and understand that we are each your unique child. Help us to know and fulfill your purpose for our lives.

We accept that we will not understand everything that happens, but we trust that you know best and that you will guide us to do your will in this world.

As your children, we pray in the name of your Son, Jesus Christ.

Amen

Your Turn

Think about some of the labels you have carried with you throughout your life. How does adding "child of God" to that list make you feel?

_____
_____
_____

What does being a child of God mean to you?

_____
_____
_____

Do you know the purpose for which God created you? If so, what is it?

_____
_____
_____

How did you come to know God's purpose for you?

_____
_____
_____

What is preventing you from living out the purpose God has for you?

_____

_____

_____

Chapter 3

Have Faith in God

What is faith?

The primary definition of faith is *complete trust or confidence in someone or something.* We have faith in many things and many people. When I walk into a dark room and flip the switch, I have faith a light will come on. When I tell my husband I want something, I have faith he'll do whatever it takes to get it for me. When I ask our neighbor to pick up our mail when we're out of town, I have faith that she'll do it.

Of course, sometimes the light doesn't come on because the bulb has burned out, the switch is broken, or the power is out. Though it doesn't happen often, there are times when my husband isn't able to give me what I want. And sometimes our neighbor forgets about our mail.

This is human faith—a belief usually founded on experience that things will function as they are supposed to and people will act as expected. There's plenty of room in human faith for an outcome different from what we expect. Biblical faith—a "faith in God"—is different.

The Biblical definition of faith is found most clearly in Hebrews 11:1: "Now faith is being sure of what we hope for and certain of what we do not see." Faith is an incredible unseen spiritual force that moves God to act—but it must come from the heart and it must be absolute.

> And without faith it is impossible to please God, because anyone who comes to him must believe that he exists and that he rewards those who earnestly seek him.
>
> *Hebrews 11:6 (NIV)*

Defining God

I want to be very clear that when I talk about God, I mean the one true God, the God of the Bible. God is not "the gods," your "higher power," the "god of your understanding," or "infinite intelligence," or whatever other word or phrase people have come up with. By the way, God is also not male or female. I use the masculine pronoun and refer to God as "father," but I do that for convenience and ease of writing and reading. The reality is that God is far beyond our human concept of gender.

God is God, and faith in the one true God is a critical key to dealing with the challenges of our life on Earth.

What Faith Is Not

Usually when we talk about faith, we focus on what it is, but to gain a true understanding of Biblical faith, you need to know what it is not.

Faith is not religion. It's not dogma or doctrine, customs, or traditions.

Faith is not mental assent. It's not intellectual agreement or simply knowing in your head that something is true.

Faith is not magic. It's not a way to manipulate God or anyone else into doing what we want when they would not otherwise be willing to do that.

Faith is not an attitude. It's not positive thinking or willing something into being simply because you want it to be so.

Faith is not mere human hope. It's not wishful thinking or desire; it's not just wanting something to be.

Though these things are generally good, they are not the faith God wants us to have in him. God doesn't want us to "hope and pray"— he wants us to pray and know. Hope is defined as a *feeling of expectation and desire for a certain thing to happen.* Hope is good for the mind and creates a condition that is conducive to faith, but it is not faith. Faith is the means by which the things we hope for are realized. It's evidence of things not seen. It's the confidence in and the assurance of the Word of God.

Have you ever heard someone say "seeing is believing," meaning that they will only believe (or have faith) in something when they can see it? That doesn't make sense. Once something exists in our human world and we can see it, we don't need faith in it. Faith lets you know something in your heart without ever seeing it with your eyes.

Believe and Obey Completely

Having faith means you believe God. Not just that you believe in God but that you believe what he says. You take him at his word, all the time, in everything. After all, if we are willing to trust God for our eternal life, we should be willing to trust him with our earthly life. Faith also leads to obedience to God's commands, and this pleases God.

People who don't believe in God will believe something else—and that something else is likely to be Satan or another personification of evil. They don't necessarily believe in Satan; they may not be devil-worshipers. Let's be clear that it's possible to believe what the devil says whether or not you believe that he actually exists. Satan is an angel who rebelled against God (even angels have free will) and took other angels with him into rebellion. Satan lies, he is motivated by hate, and he does his best to lead people into lives of sin. He's very persuasive in his attempts to convince us that we should worship him and follow his sinful ways. You don't have to believe that Satan exists to believe his messages that it's okay to lead a life that is immoral, that it's okay to be jealous, that it's okay to indulge in violent fits of rage, or that it's okay to steal, gossip or hurt others.

You may be thinking that you know none of those things is acceptable. But think about the times you've felt envious or angry, or that you didn't correct a bill that was less than it should have been, or that you repeated a juicy story and took pleasure in spreading gossip for no beneficial reason, or just did something that was hurtful. If you excused your behavior with justification or blame or even "I'm only human," you have—at least momentarily—believed what the devil says.

God doesn't want you to either believe Satan or believe in Satan. He wants us to have faith in God and worship God. He wants us to know he exists and trust what he says. I don't know of anyone who is better qualified than

> "Faith is taking the first step even when you don't see the whole staircase."
> *Martin Luther King, Jr.*

God to care for, protect, and comfort us; tell us the truth; and give us the right answers for life and eternity.

Benefits of Faith

What can faith do for you that you can't do for yourself? More than I can say. For starters, faith gives us salvation and eternal life and protects us from evil. Faith also opens the door so that healing, prosperity, peace, love, and joy can come into our lives. Faith brings answers to our prayers.

Having faith does not mean a problem-free life—far from it. Faithful or not, we all live in an imperfect world and we all must deal with pain, disappointment, and challenges. I don't know why a lot of horrible things happen. But I do know that if you have faith in God, you will find comfort and strength in that faith no matter what happens—and that may well be the biggest benefit of all.

Faith Is a Work in Progress

A common human characteristic is that when things are going well, we take credit for it, but when they're not, we blame God. True faith is knowing that God is always in control, even when it seems like things are out of control. It's easy to be faithful when things are good. It's not so easy when things are bad. We should expect our faith to be tested. You may lose material things. You may experience pain. But faith can get you through whatever you must deal with.

Let's get practical about faith. When you first believe, it's likely that your faith is not anywhere near as strong as it will eventually become. That's why it's called a faith walk—it's a journey down a long, wonderful road that takes you closer to God with every step.

I have known people who believe in God but whose faith is weak. It might be difficult to comprehend that we can believe in God, but that doesn't always mean we trust in him, and trust is the foundation of faith. There's a big difference between belief and trust. I know plenty of people who believe in God, but not all those people put their trust in him—or they only trust him sometimes.

> "I tell you the truth, if you have faith as small as a mustard seed, you can say to this mountain, 'Move from here to there' and it will move. Nothing will be impossible for you."
>
> Matthew 17:20 (NIV)

If you feel like your faith is weak, know that it doesn't have to be that way. Regardless of where you are in your walk today, you can grow and develop your faith. Here's how:

• *Read and listen to the Word of God as much as possible.* Read the Bible. Listen to an audio version when it's not practical to read. Immersing yourself in God's Word with an open heart and an open mind will strengthen your faith. Knowing God's history and the life of his people helps build your confidence in who he is. You can use this knowledge to help you reflect on how he has worked before in your own life, which will strengthen your faith in him today and tomorrow.

- *Spend time building a strong prayer life.* Praying—talking and listening to God—is one of the easiest ways to build faith. We'll talk more about prayer later.

- *Obey God.* Know how God wants you to live. As you are faithful in small things, God will reveal larger things. Obedience is a very practical way to grow faith. A lot of people have trouble with the word "obedient"—and I'm one of them. I just don't like being told what to do, especially if I'm being told to do something I don't want to do. But Jesus said, "If you love me, you will obey what I command." (John 14:15) When you love God and have faith in him, the desire to obey him comes naturally.

- *Be thankful.* Develop an attitude of gratitude. Give thanks for what you have, and don't complain about what you don't have. Look for what is right in a situation, not just what is wrong. Being consistently thankful lets you focus on the good; the benefit of that is what we think about will eventually manifest. When you focus on what you are thankful for, you will receive even more for which you can be thankful. One of the best ways to cultivate thankfulness is to keep a gratitude journal. When you start writing down what you are thankful for, you'll be surprised at how long your list is.

• *Worship.* Worship is more than prayer. In worship, you have the opportunity to express your reverence and adoration for God. Celebrate this in worship.

• *Spend time with other people of faith.* Let their faith walk strengthen yours, and as you grow, you can help others do the same. This is being part of the Body of Christ.

• *Share the Good News.* Be open about your faith and tell others how wonderful it is to let God be in control of your life. Of course, remember that there's a big difference between sharing and lecturing. You can't browbeat anyone into believing but you can show them how joyful living a Godly life can be.

• *Give love to others.* Faith works by love—the love of God and the love of one another.

Even as you work to grow your faith, you must at the same time guard against things that can weaken your faith. Ignorance, fear, doubt, discouragement, and pride are all enemies of faith. You will defeat ignorance as you increase your knowledge and understanding

> "Faith is to believe what you do not see; the reward of this faith is to see what you believe."
> *Saint Augustine*

of the Bible. Fear is an expectation that bad things will happen—and most things we fear never actually come to pass or if they do, they aren't as bad as we anticipated. Doubt challenges the truth. Discouragement weakens us and makes us vulnerable to negativity and evil influences. Pride, or the love of praise, causes your priorities and God's priorities to be out of alignment.

Knowing and understanding what can weaken your faith will help prepare you to fight back with truth. Strong faith is not insurance that you will never face challenges or struggles. Rather, it is assurance that you will never face them alone.

We need faith in God. We need it to live and to resist evil and temptation. It's much easier to have faith in God when you know him, and the easiest way to get to know him is to spend time with him. We'll talk about that in Chapter Seven. For now, just know that when we have faith, we will always find joy in the morning, every morning.

Please Pray With Me

Most Good and Gracious Lord,

Though we have never seen you, we know without a doubt you exist. Yet we confess there are times when we do doubt. We know you understand, and we ask that you help us keep our faith in you strong.

God, we know there is only enough room in our minds and hearts for one God. We ask that you come into every corner of our lives and give us the peace and comfort that only knowing you can bring.

Amen

Your Turn

How do you define faith?

_____
_____
_____

How would you describe your faith in God?

_____
_____
_____

What experiences have you had that strengthened your faith in God? Why?

_____
_____
_____

In what areas of your life do you find it most difficult to trust God?

_____
_____
_____

In what areas of your life do you find it easy to trust God?

_____
_____
_____

Chapter 4

Live in the Moment

One of the most important lessons we can learn from babies is to live in the moment.

Babies don't regret the past or worry about the future—they are concerned about right now. If they're hungry, they want to be fed. If they've got a dirty diaper, they want it changed. If some adult is saying silly things that are making them laugh, they're happy. They don't understand regret or worry until we teach it to them.

Unfortunately, once we have learned how to feel regret and worry, it's difficult to unlearn. And I will be the first to admit that what I'm about to tell you is much easier said than done. But it can be done.

Leave the Past in the Past

Take yesterday's trash out and leave it out—don't bring it back inside.

We've all got things in our pasts that, on looking back, we might do differently. But we can't go back and do things over. All we can do is move forward.

As part of letting go of the past, don't waste your time and energy on regrets and guilt. Those emotions will eat you alive and stop you from living the life God wants for you. Certainly you need to learn from your mistakes, for they give us some of our most valuable lessons. And we know that some of us have to repeat our mistakes multiple times before we get the lesson God wants us to learn. That's okay. We are fortunate that God has infinite patience with us.

Make Amends and Move On

Sometimes the only person we hurt by our mistakes is ourselves. Other times, we inflict pain on others. When that happens, we should make a sincere effort to make amends.

Making amends is one of the key parts of 12-step programs such as Alcoholics Anonymous. It's not just offering an apology, although that may be part of it. The process of making amends brings about reconciliation. To be reconciled is to restore friendship or harmony. Jesus made it possible for us to be reconciled to

God, and God wants us to be reconciled with one another. It is only after we have tried to make amends—whether or not we succeed—that can we truly put the past behind us and live in the present.

Often when we hurt people, we want to deny responsibility. We try to tell ourselves what we did wasn't wrong—or at least wasn't that bad. We excuse ourselves by claiming that the other person was too sensitive. Or we fall back on saying it was an accident, we didn't mean it, and therefore we don't have to accept responsibility for it. But until we face the situation and go to the other person as God tells us to do in the Bible, reconciliation will not happen.

> When the past calls, let it go to voicemail—it has nothing new to say.
>
> *Unknown*

Now, before you start calling or emailing everybody you've ever hurt with apologies, stop and think about what you're doing. Talk to God first. Spend time in prayer, sharing your feelings with God. Tell him you feel hurt, angry, insecure, embarrassed, or guilty, that you know you've hurt someone and you want to make it right. But you want to be sure that whatever you do will actually have the results you want and not cause more pain. Listen for God to tell you what to do and how to do it, and count on him to tell you to make the first move. I can promise you it's not likely to be an easy or comfortable move but do it anyway.

We can all learn from the Jewish holiday of Yom Kippur (Day of Atonement)—the holiest day of the Jewish year. Atonement means reconciliation, as in bringing together those who have been separated by some act. Look at the construction of the word: *at-one-ment*. Yom Kippur addresses the reconciliation of humans with God, but we can take that concept into our human relationships because God wants us to reconcile with each other.

A key part of making amends is to admit your mistakes—something that's very difficult for most of us. You've probably heard the joke: "I made a mistake once. I thought I was wrong, but I wasn't."

I happen to believe that striving for perfection is a good and worthwhile goal, one that God supports. I think too many people use excuses like "I'm only human" and "Everybody makes mistakes" to avoid making the effort of doing their best. Yes, we are only human, but we are made in God's image and God is perfect. Of course, part of God's perfection is his never-ending patience with us. But to get back to the issue of making amends:

When you are admitting your mistakes, be humble; don't get defensive, make excuses, or try to shift the blame. Own up to whatever you might have done. If you're dealing with an ongoing conflict, attack the problem, not the person. It's unrealistic to expect everyone to agree on everything, so emphasize reconciliation, not resolution. You can make amends and re-establish a relationship, even if you are unable to completely resolve your differences. Remember, we can always agree to disagree.

You may not always have a face-to-face reconciliation with the other person. There will be times that's simply not possible—the other person may not be living, or you may not be able to make contact for some reason, or contact would cause more harm than good. Pray about this, consider talking with a skilled counselor if necessary—just be sure that as you work to make amends and achieve reconciliation that you don't inadvertently do something else for which you'll need to make amends.

> "The Christian life is not a constant high. I have my moments of deep discouragement. I have to go to God in prayer with tears in my eyes, and say, 'O God, forgive me,' or 'Help me.'"
>
> *Billy Graham*

One final thought on making amends: It's more for your benefit than for the other person. Once you have either successfully made amends, or tried your best to do so but have not been successful, let it go and move on so you can live in the present instead of being bogged down by the past.

FINDING JOY IN THE MORNING

Don't Worry about Tomorrow

The easiest way to deal with worry is to understand what it is: Worrying is just praying for what you don't want to happen. It's a waste of time and energy because you're just imagining what may never happen. And worry makes us sick, physically and mentally.

You've probably heard about people who had nervous breakdowns because they worked too much or too hard. "Nervous breakdown" is a nonmedical term that is used to describe a situation so distressful that a person has become unable to function normally in day-to-day life. The truth is that nervous breakdowns come from too much worry, not too much work.

Scottish historian and essayist Thomas Carlyle wrote: "Our main business is not to see what lies dimly at a distance but to do what lies clearly at hand." You don't know what's going to happen tomorrow, so don't worry about it. God doesn't want you to—that's evident by the language of the prayer Jesus taught the disciples to say: "Give us this day our daily bread." All the prayer asks for is bread for today—it doesn't say anything about the bread you had yesterday, whether it was fresh and flavorful or stale and moldy. It doesn't say anything about the bread you'll have tomorrow. The prayer asks for today's bread only. That's all you need.

Here's a way to put worry in its proper perspective: If you get the flu, chances are you'll be very ill for a couple of weeks, and then you'll recover. An average of 5 to 20 percent of the U.S. population gets the flu every year; most recover without long-term effects. Over the 30-year period from 1976 to 2006, estimates of flu-associated deaths in the United States range from a low of about 3,000 to a high of about 49,000 people. When you put that in perspective of the total population and other causes of death, not very many people die from the flu. Even so, at the beginning of flu season, you're hard pressed to go a full day without seeing or hearing something either urging you to get a flu vaccine or telling you that the shot is available wherever you happen to be. A flu-related death in your area is likely to make headlines. Even so, for most of us, the flu is not much more than an inconvenience, yet there are massive annual campaigns to make you aware of how to either avoid it or at least lessen its impact.

Now let's compare the flu to worry. Worry stirs up negative emotions and keeps reinforcing them. In response, your body experiences surges

> "Many people feel so pressured by the expectations of others that it causes them to be frustrated, miserable and confused about what they should do. But there is a way to live a simple, joy-filled, peaceful life, and the key is learning how to be led by the Holy Spirit, not the traditions or expectations of man."
>
> *Joyce Meyer*

of stress hormones and releases chemical stimulants to help you prepare to either fight or flee. Your blood pressure goes up, your digestive system slows down, your heart pounds, your breathing becomes shallow, and your stomach muscles contract. Stress compromises your immune system and generates excessive demand on your cardiovascular system. The greater your stress level, the more likely you are to catch a cold or another infectious disease. Stress speeds the metastasis of cancer, worsens asthma, causes stomach ulcers, and is correlated with arteriosclerosis (hardening of the arteries) and myocardial infarction (heart attack). Yet how often are you warned about the dangers of worry? Instead, doctors treat the symptoms of worry—high blood pressure, depression, anxiety, heart disease, even obesity—without addressing the true underlying cause of those often life-threatening conditions.

> "When I look back on all these worries, I remember the story of the old man who said on his deathbed that he had had a lot of trouble in his life, most of which had never happened."
>
> Winston Churchill

Get a Worry Vaccine

I'm not going to tell you whether or not to get vaccinated against the flu or any other disease. I am, however, going to suggest that you vaccinate yourself against worry by understanding what it is and how it can harm you, and refusing to let it control you.

If you're worried about something, try these three easy steps to deal with it:

1. Do a complete and honest analysis of the situation and come up with a worst-case scenario of what might happen. Could you lose your job? Money? A loved one? Maybe just be embarrassed or inconvenienced? What is the absolute worst thing that could happen as a result of what you're worrying about?

2. Reconcile yourself to accepting the worst-case scenario if it happens. Know that God will be with you every step of the way and you will survive.

3. Concentrate on trying to improve the worst-case scenario that you have already accepted. Ask God to help you do what you can to prevent the worst case from happening.

Most of the time, what ends up actually happening is not anywhere near as bad as what we envisioned. Even when there might be some validity to our worries, investing time and energy in worry detracts from our ability to figure out and then do what might prevent the worst case from happening or at least reduce its impact.

Another way to deal with worry is to ask yourself two simple questions:
What am I worrying about?
What can I do about it?

Write your answers down. Then stop worrying and implement the action in your second answer. And if there's nothing you can do, why worry? Turn it over to God—as the saying goes, he's going to be up all night, anyway.

Be Comfortable with Not Knowing

We do not know what the future holds, only God does. That's a basic truth we must come to terms with.

There's an old parable that illustrates this. When a farmer's ox died, he went to the village wise man and said frantically, "My ox has died, and I have no animal to help me plow my field. Isn't this the worst thing that could possibly happen?"

The wise man said, "Maybe so, maybe not."

The farmer returned to his home and told his neighbors that the wise man had gone mad. Surely this was the worst thing that could have happened. Why couldn't he see that?

The next day a strong, young horse appeared on the man's farm. It didn't seem to belong to anyone, so the farmer claimed it. He was overjoyed. Not only had plowing the field never been easier, but he now had a horse to ride.

He went back to the wise man to apologize. "You were right," he said. "Losing my ox wasn't the worst thing. It was actually a blessing in disguise. I would never have captured my new horse had that not happened. You must agree that this is the best thing that could have happened."

Once again, the wise man said, "Maybe so, maybe not."

The farmer again thought the wise man was crazy.

A few days later, the farmer's son was riding the horse and was thrown off. He broke his leg and would not be able to help harvest the crop.

"Oh, no," thought the farmer. "Now we will starve to death." He went to the wise man and demanded, "How did you know that capturing the horse was not a good thing? You were right again. My son is injured and will not be able to help with the crop. I am sure this is the worst thing that could possibly have happened. You must agree this time."

Once again the wise man was calm and compassionate as he simply said, "Maybe so, maybe not."

The farmer was enraged by what he saw as the wise man's ignorance. He stormed back to

> Therefore I tell you, do not worry about your life, what you will eat or drink; or about your body, what you will wear. Is not life more than food, and the body more than clothes? ... Therefore do not worry about tomorrow, for tomorrow will worry about itself. Each day has enough trouble of its own.
> *Matthew 6:25, 34 (NIV)*

the village.

The next day, troops arrived to take every able-bodied man to help fight the war that had just broken out. The farmer's son was the only young man in the village who didn't have to go. He would live while the others would likely die.

In all these situations, the farmer wanted the wise man to make a commitment no human could make. The wise man's wisdom manifested in his refusal to predict the future. We don't know what's going to happen. We don't know if the best or the worst of our lives is ahead or behind us. We also don't know when we're in the middle of a situation how it's going to turn out. So just relax, don't worry, and trust God.

> "Drag your thoughts away from your troubles... by the ears, by the heels, or any other way you can manage it."
>
> Mark Twain

Don't Worry, Do Plan

There is, of course, a difference between worry and planning. Worry is destructive; planning is constructive.

We should plan for the future. We should save money so we have financial resources when we need them. We should get an education so we can enjoy the career of our choice. All of that takes planning. On a smaller scale, we should plan our schedules so that we can get things accomplished. Even as we live in the present and focus our energy on the now, we know that tomorrow will come and we should be ready for it. But the key is preparation, not anxiety.

Do things like "breakfast is the most important meal of the day" and "start your day with a nutritious breakfast" sound familiar? It's good advice we should take a step further: Start each day by nourishing your physical body and by exercising your spiritual muscles. Begin each day by letting go of yesterday, turning today over to God, and not worrying about tomorrow.

If you do that, does it mean your life will be perfect? No. But it will be a lot better than if you poison yourself with regrets about the past and worry about the future.

There's a message I like that makes its way around the internet periodically that reads: "Good morning, this is God. I'll be handling all your problems today. I will not need your help, so relax and have a great day."

It's a perfect reminder of who's in charge.

Please Pray With Me

Dear God,

Thank you for yesterday, today, and tomorrow.
Help us to leave yesterday in the past, live
fully today, and not worry about tomorrow.
This is the way to live as a true child of God.

Amen

Your Turn

Within the last month, how much time have you spent regretting things that have happened in the past?

_____
_____
_____

Think of something that worried you to the point that you spent at least five hours thinking about it. What sort of scenarios did you envision in your worries, and how closely did they compare with what really happened?

_____
_____
_____

Think about someone you've hurt. What should you do to make amends?

_____
_____
_____

Consider the difference between worrying and planning. Think about a situation that caused you to worry. What happened? Think about a situation you planned for. What happened?

_____
_____
_____

Chapter 5

Understand the Importance of Community

We are not meant to live alone or exist in isolation.

Human beings are made to live in community. We need intellectual, emotional, and physical interaction with other people. That's why solitary confinement is such a horrible punishment and effective method of torture. It's why babies need to be held and cuddled—we know if they're not, they often fail to thrive.

That God wants us to be part of a community is just one of his many gifts to us. He has given us one another for fellowship and support and, in his infinite wisdom, designed us to bring out the best in each other, even in the face of tremendous adversity. Yes, we do need solitude—Jesus regularly went off by himself to pray and came back rested and recharged, and we should follow his example—but we also need people. We need family and friends. And when I say "family and friends," I'm not talking about common genetics or social status. I'm talking about relationships.

A few years ago, my husband and I received a frantic call from a woman we knew from church and had become close friends with. Her mother had retired a few months earlier and moved in with her. Our friend came home from work one day and found her mother dead. Now, her mother's health wasn't great and, in some ways, her death wasn't a total surprise. But there had been no specific warnings; our friend just walked in the door and saw her mother's body on the floor. I can only imagine the shock she felt.

> "No one can whistle a symphony. It takes a whole orchestra to play it."
>
> H.E. Luccock

My husband and I immediately headed to her house, making calls to other church members while en route. Because the death was unattended, the police were there. An officer who knew there were no other family members in the area watched as a steady stream of people arrived to comfort and help. He already knew that our friend had no other blood relatives nearby, and I heard him ask, "Are these friends of yours?" She replied with a certain degree of pride in her voice, "They're my church family."

More than a church family, they were God's family. They were people who had initially come together because of a shared faith and through that faith built relationships with one another. Our friend is a capable, intelligent woman. Could she have made it through that crisis on her own? I don't know, but she didn't have to. That's really the point of the story. This is what God wants for us—he wants us to be part of a community, of a family. And it's not just about getting through the tough times, it's about enjoying the good times together, it's about working and growing together.

Needing other people does not mean you're weak. On the contrary, it makes you strong. What is impossible for one person to do alone becomes easy when many are involved.

It Takes Effort and Engagement

You need relationships, but here's the catch: Relationships require effort and engagement.

Is it easy to maintain close relationships with your family and friends, especially the ones you don't live with? Absolutely not. It takes work, a deliberate effort, and time—and people don't always appreciate what you're trying to do. Do it anyway.

What you need to do is figure out a plan for building and maintaining relationships that works for you and commit to it. It's so easy to call that person tomorrow—and tomorrow never comes. Or to say, "We have to get together sometime," then wait for someone else to take the initiative, and it never happens. Or to think that you don't need to say "I love you" because the other person knows you do. They may know it, but they need to hear it—often.

Consider doing an annual relationship review. Pick a day every year that you sit down and look at your relationships—family, friends, professional colleagues, neighbors, even casual acquaintances. How are your relationships? Healthy and happy? Or troubled and tense? What are you doing that's positive and you could do more of? What are you doing that's negative and could be changed or improved?

With that review, make a list of things you can do to strengthen your relationships and start doing them. It might be just calling some-

> "In poverty and other misfortunes of life, true friends are a sure refuge. The young they keep out of mischief; to the old they are a comfort and aid in their weakness, and those in the prime of life they incite to noble deeds."
> — *Aristotle*

one you haven't talked to in a while. It might be reaching out to help in a more tangible way. Your goal is to identify and correct the minor issues before they escalate into big problems. Think about this: You probably take your car in for regular maintenance—aren't your relationships worth at least a similar investment?

The Role of Technology in Community

I don't need to tell you we are living in a time of mind-boggling technological advances, with some of the most amazing communication tools at our fingertips. I'm the first to admit I'd have a hard time getting along without my cell phone, and one of the easiest ways to get a short message to me is by texting. I get hundreds of emails a day. I'm active on LinkedIn, Facebook, and Twitter.

> Greater love has no one than this, that he lay down his life for his friends. You are my friends if you do what I command.
>
> *John 15:13-14 (NIV)*

It's a sad paradox that even as technology has given us an incredible array of communication options, it has become harder than ever to stay truly connected. Having hundreds or thousands of "friends" or "followers" on the latest social media platform isn't enough to meet our deep human need to be part of a community. In fact, spending too much time "communicating" electronically rather than in person can lead to depression and other problems.

You should use all the communication tools you have—just be sure you are truly connecting because that's a fundamental necessity of maintaining relationships.

Families and Friends

Families are not perfect, but they're still your family, and they always will be. At the same time, the old saying that you choose your friends but not your family is absolutely true. So is the saying that you can tell a lot about people by the company they keep.

The Bible has a lot to say about friends and friendship. The measure of our true wealth is in our friends. God wants us to have friends, and he wants us to be a friend.

It's important to understand what true friendship is—and isn't. Friendship is not about using other people to get what you want. It's not calling someone only when you're in need. It's not encouraging someone to make a bad decision. It's not promoting any sort of poor behavior. Friendship means unconditional love and honesty (with a healthy share of tact). It

> "At the end of your life, you will never regret not having passed one more test, not winning one more verdict or not closing one more deal. You will regret time not spent with a husband, a friend, a child, or a parent."
>
> *Barbara Bush*

means accepting people for who they are and loving them, warts and all. It means caring enough to tell them the truth when you think they're making a mistake. And it means being there for them when they make a mistake and need someone to help them pick up the pieces.

The way to gain friends is to offer your own friendship first. Do it without calculation, without expecting anything in return. Just be a friend. You don't have to give lavish gifts; you just have to be there. The greatest gift you can give someone is yourself—the gift of your time, listening, caring, helping. Will some people take advantage of you? Maybe, but don't let that stop you. Instead, focus on your own spirit of giving, not the taker. You are doing the right thing, and God will bless your efforts.

True friendship freely given and gratefully received is one of life's greatest gifts.

Get Professional Help When You Need It

As important as your family and friends are, there will be times when they are not enough. Recognize those situations and get professional help when you need it.

Professional help comes in many forms. It could come from a health care provider, a counselor, a lawyer, a financial advisor—I could go on, but you get my point. Sometimes the need for some types of professional assistance is clear: When you're physically sick, you go to the doctor. When you're involved in a legal situation, you consult with a lawyer. Sometimes it's not so clear: Can you really handle that do-it-yourself home repair project or do you need an expert? And then there's the special challenge of when you're struggling with emotional and/or spiritual issues. Sometimes you're just having a bad day, and venting to a friend is all you need, but sometimes you need to seek out a therapist or a minister.

God wants us to pray and ask for his help, but often he sends that help in human form. Be watching for it and ready to receive it.

Don't Sweat the Small Stuff

Relationships are often destroyed by things that don't really matter. Those things might seem important now, but are they really?

When you're dealing with a relationship issue, imagine yourself 10 or 20 years in the future, looking back on whatever situation is causing problems today. Maybe because of those problems you haven't spoken to the person or people involved—friends or family members—in decades. You've missed major milestones in each other's lives—births, deaths, marriages, baptisms, graduations. How proud are you of how you handled the situation? How important does the issue seem now?

If whatever it was won't matter in 20 years,

how much can it really matter today? And if it doesn't matter, let it go.

I realize there are some conflicts that really are important—they matter a lot today, and they'll matter in the future. If you honestly apply this technique and believe the issue is still significant, you need to figure out a path to resolution. Earlier we talked about making amends, and that may be what you need to do. If someone has injured you, you may need to forgive—and that's not easy. In the next chapter, we're going to talk more about forgiveness.

Please Pray With Me

Father,

We praise and thank you for the wonderful gift of relationships. We ask that you be with our friends and family today, that they would be filled by your Holy Spirit. Guide, comfort, and strengthen them. Keep them in our thoughts and hearts. Help us let them know how much we love and care for them. Give us the wisdom and sensitivity we need to keep our relationships strong, to be the parents, the children, the spouses, and friends that you would have us be. Let us be the tangible expression of your love in the lives of those around us who desperately seek comfort, belonging, and hope.

We pray in your most holy name.

Amen

Your Turn

What makes you uncomfortable about needing other people?

___
___
___

How do you keep in touch with the people you care about?

___
___
___

Do you find it easy to say "I love you" to the people you love? Why or why not?

___
___
___

Think of three people with whom you need to reconcile.

___
___
___

What steps can you take right now to mend those relationships and begin the process of reconciliation?

Chapter 6

Practice Forgiveness

God forgives us—how can we do any less for each other?

Even as we may understand that on an intellectual level, forgiveness is one of the hardest things for us to do.

When you forgive, you make a conscious decision to let go of hurt, resentment, anger, and thoughts of revenge. You can't undo what happened, and you don't have to forget it. Instead, you make a choice to focus on other positive parts of your life and relationships. When you have been harmed, forgiveness is the kindest thing you can do for yourself.

Is forgiving easier said than done? Yes. But we don't do it alone. It takes Christ working through us to give us strength.

FINDING JOY IN THE MORNING

Something very important to remember about forgiveness is it's a process, not an event. It's a choice we make, and sometimes we have to make it many times. You don't just do it, and it's done. You can't always forgive instantly and never have to deal with it again. If someone has done you a terrible wrong, you may have to make the choice every day to forgive them.

It's also important for you to come to terms with this reality: How you feel about someone else does not injure that person at all. The only person you hurt when you harbor hatred or other negative feelings is yourself. The Aramaic word for forgive means to untie. When you forgive, you untie yourself from the hurt, pain, anger, and burden you carry from that, and free yourself to live a successful and happy life.

> "When you forgive, you in no way change the past, but you sure do change the future."
>
> *Bernard Meltzer*

In the process of forgiving, take the time to look at the situation and identify the good things that happened as a result of it. What did you learn? What were the positive outcomes? Ask God to do more than simply help you let go, ask him to show you how your life will be better for the experience.

Here's another perspective: When things happen to you, they're not always completely about you. Did someone else come to your aid and have an opportunity to serve in some way?

Think about it: Were others blessed because they were able to help you when you were going through a bad time? That could be a reason to forgive whoever was responsible for your difficulties.

One more angle you need to consider is this: If you're suffering because of someone else's actions, keep in mind that the person who wronged you, who you may see as an enemy, is someone else's child, parent, spouse, or sibling—and is, as you are, a child of God. Wish that person well. And yes, it's quite okay for you to wish that person to be well somewhere that's not in close proximity to you. The blessing you offer will come back to you multiplied.

> "To forgive is to set a prisoner free and discover that the prisoner was you."
> Lewis B. Smedes

You've probably heard one or more versions of the saying that failing to forgive and holding grudges is like drinking poison and hoping the other person dies. The only person hurt when you don't forgive is you. And the person who benefits the most when you forgive is you.

Accept that you can forgive and still feel hurt. When we've been injured, it takes time to heal—and the deeper the wound, the longer the healing takes. But you can't even begin to heal until you forgive.

Keep Doing It

As I was leaving church one Sunday after hearing a sermon on forgiveness, I said to the pastor, "Does the fact that I'm still ticked off about something mean I haven't forgiven?" I was smiling, trying to keep my question light. He smiled back, but said seriously, "It means you still have some work to do."

What I've come to understand is that even after I forgive, sometimes the negative feelings will bubble back up and I'll need to forgive again. It's common for us to have to forgive the same person for the same offense over and over. That's why we call it practicing forgiveness—even when we master it, we have to keep practicing to maintain our skills.

When you forgive, simply forgive. Don't demand punishment or retribution. Don't worry about justice. Those things won't change what happened and they won't make you feel better. Remember, forgiveness isn't about the other person, it's about you. And in keeping with that understanding, accept apologies at face value. Whether they're sincere or not is not your problem.

> "Forgiveness is an act of the will, and the will can function regardless of the temperature of the heart."
>
> *Corrie Ten Boom*

Finally, understand that forgiving does not mean forgetting. If someone has harmed you and they're likely to do it again, you need to remember that so you take whatever steps are necessary to protect yourself. This is particularly important in situations such as domestic violence, where harmful behaviors are often repetitive. But it can apply to other situations as well. For example, you can forgive an addict for stealing from you but take steps to prevent another theft. There's a healthy difference between letting go of grudges and remembering what happened so we don't allow it to happen again. God wants us to forgive, but he doesn't want us to repeatedly put ourselves in a position where we can be harmed. Forgiveness should bring you peace, not pain.

Please Pray With Me

Dear God,

We have turned our lives over to you. We ask that you help make us the best we can be. We are powerless over the issues of our lives and the conduct of others. We surrender our life and issues to you and see the guidance, comfort, and strength of the Holy Spirit. It is only through that surrender that we are able to forgive and to find peace in the process.

We are listening now to hear your Word, and we ask that you keep us on track as we go out to do your will.

Amen

Your Turn

Who do you need to forgive?

_____
_____
_____

Have you had the experience of having forgiven someone only to have the negative feelings return? How did you deal with it?

_____
_____
_____

Chapter 7

Stay On Track (Close to God)

Once you ask God to come into your heart and you turn your life over to him, staying close to him is easy, right?

Wrong.

Staying close to God takes conscious effort and work just like any other relationship. The temptation of the world will always be there, trying to get between you and God, pulling you away from God and toward false belief and immoral behavior.

For most of us, moving away from God isn't something we do in leaps; it's something we do inch by inch. When we get busy and stop taking time to pray every day, we've moved away a few inches. Good things happen, and we take credit instead of praising God—now we've moved a few feet. We stop studying and reading the Bible—and now we're yards off track. The next thing we know, we're a mile off track and not sure how to get back where we belong.

The good news is getting back on track isn't difficult. In fact, it's often a lot easier to get back on track than it is to stay there in the first place. All it takes is recognizing that you got off track, that God didn't move—you did. And all you have to do to get close to God again is to want to be there. But if you are going to be able to deal with the challenges of life, you need to stay close to God. Don't keep ricocheting back and forth. When you move away from God, even a little bit, you open the door for evil.

> Oh, the depth of the riches of the wisdom and knowledge of God!
> Romans 11:33 (NIV)

Part of staying close to God is relying on God. Our culture teaches self-reliance, and that's not a bad thing in an earthly way. Certainly if we are able, we should take care of ourselves rather than depend on someone else to do it for us. But beneath our ability to live in the world (having a job, caring for our families, being good stewards of our resources), reliance on God is essential if we are to find joy in the morning.

You've probably heard that God will never

give us more than we can handle, but that's actually not true. God will give us more than we can handle because he wants us to turn to him to get through it. He will give us strength, wisdom, and comfort if we just ask for it—and often even when we don't.

When you are in pain, either emotional or physical or both, and you don't understand why God is allowing it to happen, it's natural to want to push him out. Yet inviting him in, staying close to him even as you struggle, letting him do the work, is what gives you the strength to win the battle. It's what lets you find joy in the morning.

People who live in a state of consistent peace, no matter what sort of turmoil is swirling around them, do that because they understand the need to stay on God's track, and they know how to do it. They have well-developed, strong spiritual muscles.

> "Being a Christian is more than just an instantaneous conversion—it is a daily process whereby you grow to be more and more like Christ."
>
> *Billy Graham*

Exercise Your Spiritual Muscles

Just as your body needs exercise to stay healthy and be able to perform, your spirit needs regular exercise to stay healthy and close to God. Spiritual exercise comes in the form of prayer, study, service, and worship.

Although God accepts us as we are, he

doesn't want us to remain that way. He wants us to grow in our faith, and that growth is a process. It's like learning to ride a bicycle: Sometimes you fall off, and even after you know how to ride really well, you'll still occasionally fall off. Just ask Lance Armstrong, seven-time Tour de France winner: He's had plenty of falls, many of them long after he had earned the title of one of the best cyclists in the world. Of course, his worst fall was not from his bicycle, it was from his pedestal when it became known that he had succumbed to temptation and cheated—but that's another issue. The point for now is that no matter how deep your faith is, your spiritual growth path will have curves and obstacles of varying degrees along the way.

Another analogy is to think of yourself and your faith like a house: When you accept Jesus Christ into your life, you become spotless, shiny, and clean for that moment—just like a house that's been thoroughly scrubbed. But it doesn't mean

> One day Jesus was praying in a certain place. When he finished, one of his disciples said to him, "Lord, teach us to pray, just as John taught his disciples." He said to them, "When you pray, say: 'Father, hallowed be your name, your kingdom come. Give us each day our daily bread. Forgive us our sins, for we also forgive everyone who sins against us. And lead us not into temptation.'"
>
> *Luke 11:1-4 (NIV)*

you're never going to have to clean your house again. A house is going to get dirty just by being lived in, and you'll need to clean it. Just by being alive, you're going to be exposed to negativity and temptation, and you'll need to clean your spiritual house. The most effective way to keep your spiritual house clean is with these spiritual exercises.

Prayer

Many people find it awkward, even difficult, to pray. I think it's because we know God is so awesome that we're intimidated—but we shouldn't be. God wants us to come to him in prayer, to praise him, thank him, tell him what we want and need, ask him to intercede in situations that are of concern to us, and, of course, to listen to him.

If you don't feel comfortable or confident in your ability to pray, you're not alone. Even the disciples asked Jesus how to pray, and when they did, he taught them what we have come to know as the Lord's Prayer. If you feel awkward when you go to God in prayer, try the ACTS format, which stands for adoration, confession, thanksgiving, and supplication. Every time you pray, consciously try to include each element.

Adoration: Praise God for who he is—your heavenly Father, creator of the universe, our great and awesome God. You're not telling him anything he doesn't already know; you are reminding yourself of his wonderful majesty and putting yourself in a prayerful frame of mind.

Confession: Tell God about the sins you have committed and ask for forgiveness. Again, what you say here won't be news to God—he knows what you've done. But it will show him that you know and understand, that you are repentant, and that you want his help in overcoming your sins. Be specific; don't just ask for blanket forgiveness. Take the time to recall and reflect on specific sins and their consequences. For example, if you were rude to someone or gossiped about another, confess what you did and acknowledge that your behavior hurt someone else.

> "Prayer reminds me it's not just about me. It's about all the people with whom I share this planet, and all of whom God has created, and all of whom he cares just as much about as he cares about me."
>
> Mike Huckabee

Thanksgiving: Thank God for what he has done for you, your loved ones, and the world. This shows God you are paying attention to his work and that you are grateful. As with confession, be specific in thanksgiving. Of course, thank him for the major things—health, a new job, or a rescue from a dangerous situation. But also thank him for the mundane things, such as a convenient parking place, beautiful weather, even the item you found on sale.

Supplication: This is humbly asking God for

things both material and spiritual. Ask not only for yourself but for others as well. Don't put limits on these requests because there is no limit to what God can do. Do you want a new house or car? Ask God for it. Is someone you love facing a health situation and in need of healing? Ask God for it. Are you or someone you care about a student who is studying for an important test, an athlete training for a big game, or a salesperson preparing for a critical presentation? Ask God for help in achieving the desired outcome. Do you need to make an important decision? Ask God to show you what he wants you to do. Do you want an opportunity to share God's Word? Ask God to put someone who needs to hear his wisdom in your life. As you ask God for what you want, let him know you understand you are powerless without him, and that he holds the key to everything.

> Prayer is the vehicle by which burdens change shoulders.
>
> *Unknown*

There is also the ACTIS method, which stands for adoration, confession, thanksgiving, intercession, and supplication. The acronym isn't quite as clever, but it can make your prayer time even richer. Prayers of intercession are when you pray for others—family, friends, co-workers, even strangers. The Bible is full of examples of intercessory prayer; perhaps the most powerful is when Jesus prayed for those who crucified him.

When and Where?

I believe our prayer life is richest when it combines structured, scheduled prayer and casual, spontaneous conversations with God. Prayer is a wonderful way to start your day. Set aside some quiet time every morning, ideally in a private place, where you can talk with God. Of course, this shouldn't be the only time during the day that you pray. I know many business leaders who open their meetings with prayer. Saying a blessing before meals, even something brief, is a good way to remind yourself of who is in charge of your life. And, of course, we can always pray when something unexpected happens and we need God's help.

God doesn't just hear our prayers at designated times and in a specific format; he hears them all the time, in all formats. Try pausing periodically throughout your day, even if it's just for a few seconds, and use that time to pray, to thank God for a blessing, to ask God for help in a challenging situation, or to confess and ask forgiveness for a sin. It takes some practice and discipline, but once you make it a habit, you'll find that your life will be greatly enriched in more ways that you can conceive.

Do you have to get down on your knees when you pray? No. God hears you whatever your posture is. But you may find it helpful if you have a special position or place where you go for your regular prayers. Just know that you can pray any time, any place, in any position, and God hears you.

Pray for Others

There is nothing that comforts me more than knowing that people are praying for me. My husband is always praying for me, and I know there are others who pray for me every day. And I treasure the opportunity to provide that comfort for others by praying for them

> And pray in the Spirit on all occasions with all kinds of prayers and requests.
> *Ephesians 6:18 (NIV)*

When you pray for people, pray *for* them, not *about* them. Ask God to guide them and help them be closer to him, not to fix them. If you truly believe someone else needs to change, share your feelings with God and ask him to handle it. Remember, you're not in charge of their lives—God is. And God doesn't need you to tell him how to do his job.

What Prayer Is Not

Just as we talked about what faith is and isn't, it is equally as important to understand what prayer is and is not. Prayer is not meditation, self-talk, or positive affirmations. Certainly there is nothing wrong with these activities—in fact, they are very worthwhile, but they're not prayer.

Prayer is also not a superficial recitation of words that have no meaning to you. If you're going to incorporate prayers that others have written, such as the ones in this book, take your time and consider each word and what it means. And edit those prayers if you need to.

Finally, prayer is not a way to manipulate God (you don't have enough power to do that!). Prayer is a conversation with God, one that is done purposefully, reverently, and humbly.

Even though you pray every day, will there be times when it seems as though God is not listening to you or he is not answering your prayers? Of course. Sometimes God's answer is "no," sometimes it's "not now," and sometimes it's "I have something far better in mind for you." Remember, God's time is not our time. God has reasons for what he does and doesn't do that are far beyond our ability to understand. Continue praying, and keep your heart and mind open to what God wants you to hear.

> "No one is a firmer believer in the power of prayer than the devil; not that he practices it, but he suffers from it."
>
> Guy H. King

Study

No matter where you are on your faith journey, whether you're a skeptic, a new believer, or a lifelong Christian, God wants you to grow. He wants you to study, understand, and become mature in your faith. He wants you to know his Word and to make decisions in your life that are consistent with what the Bible says. Remember: the Bible is God's Word, and God's Word is the most powerful thing in the universe.

The Bible isn't something you read once and set aside, like you would a novel, a business guide, or some other contemporary book that you might get one or two good ideas from. It's a book you should study, which means you read it again and again, ask questions, seek understanding, and write down your thoughts.

> "The Bible is one of the greatest blessings bestowed by God on the children of men. It has God for its author; salvation for its end, and truth without any mixture for its matter. It is all pure."
>
> *John Locke*

In John 14:15, Jesus said, "If you love me, you will obey what I command." The only way we can obey what Jesus commands is to know what Jesus commands. And the only way to know is to study the Bible.

Studying the Bible is not like studying your least-favorite subject in school. It's more like learning about a hobby that fascinates you or a sport you enjoy. While it takes effort, it's not unpleasant work—it's joyful. One of the most exciting things about the Bible is that it will speak to you differently each time you read it—

it's never boring, and it always has answers. What's more, a solid understanding of the Bible gives you the knowledge you need to defend your faith with clear, theologically sound answers to questions and challenges.

If you've never studied the Bible, you may find the idea intimidating. You may wonder when you'll have the time because your schedule is already jam-packed. You may, for whatever reason, be reluctant to join a Sunday School class or mid-week Bible study. That's okay. We all learn differently. What works for me may or may not work for you. What works for you may or may not work for someone else. What's important is that you figure out how you can best study the Word of God so you can mature spiritually. Ask God to show you the best way for you to learn and grow.

> What does not begin with God will end in failure.
>
> *Unknown*

Service

Service has two main components that often overlap: One is to share the Word of God, and the other is to help others who are in need.

In Matthew 28:19-20, a passage known as the Great Commission, Jesus was very specific: "Therefore go and make disciples of all nations, baptizing them in the name of the Father and of the Son and of the Holy Spirit, and teaching them to obey everything I have commanded you." To me, this is a no-brainer. My faith gives me so much joy that I want to share it with as many people as possible. It is just too wonderful to keep to myself.

The Bible also very specifically says that we should help others, and we can do that in a variety of ways. Each of us has been blessed with spiritual gifts that God wants us to use in his service to glorify him. We don't all need to head off to a poverty-stricken third world country to feed the hungry and care for the sick—although certainly that's what many of us are called to do. I'm not one of those people. In fact, I often say that God uses my gifts in places that have hot showers and flush toilets. Remember, we are all part of the Body of Christ, and we have different functions and different gifts. There are plenty of other ways we can do effective service work. Ask God what he wants you to do, and he'll show you.

> Then the King will say, "I'm telling the solemn truth: Whenever you did one of these things to someone overlooked or ignored, that was me—you did it to me."
> Matthew 25:40 (MSG)

Worship

God wants us to worship him and him alone. The act of praising God through worship helps us remember that God is in control of our lives, and we can surrender to him. It reminds us that there is something greater than us out there—something more than just what impacts us. Worship helps us exercise our spiritual muscles in a way nothing else can.

Worship is important to God—so much so that the Old Testament goes into great detail explaining how to worship God. And because worship is important to God, it should be important to us.

Do you have to go to church to worship? No, but the Bible does tell us that we are to worship together. When you read the New Testament, you'll see that people came together in groups and worshiped in one another's homes. Did they also have their private time for devotion, study, and prayer? I'm sure they did. So did Jesus—that's documented in Scripture. But even though they had their solitary moments, they worshiped together in community.

> "Disciples are not people who never doubt. They doubt and worship. They doubt and serve. They doubt and help each other with their doubts. They doubt and practice faithfulness. They doubt and wait for their doubt one day to be turned into knowing."
>
> John Ortberg

There are three reasons to worship God:

One, he commands it. The Bible tells us this over and over.

Two, he deserves it. Only God is holy. He is the all-powerful creator whose goodness, kindness, mercy, and love surpass our human understanding.

Three, we need to do it. If we do not worship God, we will probably worship something else—and that would be a violation of his commandments.

By today's standards, I'm a traditional worshiper. I like a choir in robes singing the hymns I remember from childhood (even though I didn't go to church very often when I was a kid). I want a degree of formality and ritual in my Sunday morning service. I don't want some guy in jeans with his shirttail out bringing me a message; I want a pastor in a robe in a pulpit preaching a sermon. Of course, I want that sermon and all of the other elements of the service to contain a meaningful message—it's not just about the ceremony, it's about what each element means.

> God is spirit, and those who worship him must worship in spirit and in truth.
> *John 4:24 (NRSV)*

Even as I recognize my own worship preferences, I understand that others prefer to worship in a more casual setting with a band instead of a choir and plenty of visual aids. I don't think God cares about the accouterments as long as your heart is in the right place. I know people who attend mega-churches with tens of thousands of members and the latest technology; I know people who belong to mid-sized churches that are part of mainline denominations; and I know people who are part of very small independent congregations (my cousin calls hers "church in a closet" because they meet in a school, and their equipment is stored in a closet and has to be dragged out, set up, and put away every Sunday).

My point is: Do not allow discussions of various worship styles to get in the way of the actual act of worship. Worship styles have always varied from culture to culture and century to century. It doesn't matter if you worship in quiet stillness or in noisy motion—what matters is that you worship and you do it regularly.

Let God Move You

As I've already said, if you have felt close to God in the past but you're not feeling close to him now, it's because you moved—God is where he always is. If you've pushed God out of your life, tell him you want him back. And if you're new to the faith, tell God you want to stay close to him every minute of every day.

If you let him, God will do all the heavy lifting to bring you close to him, whatever it takes for your particular circumstances. Just ask. Try it. You've got nothing to lose and absolutely everything to gain.

Please Pray With Me

Dear God,

You are our heavenly Father, and you have given us all things in life. There is no way we could take credit for the successes we have had. We give you all the praise, honor, and glory for all that we have.

We lift up our lives to you today and pray that your will, not ours, be done.

We ask that you put someone in our lives today whom we can minister to, someone we can help to understand the amazing peace and joy that comes from knowing you.

You are the God who hears all our prayers, who sees everything we do, who knows what's in our hearts.

Amen

Your Turn

What new actions can you take this week to exercise your spiritual muscles?

___
___
___

Which of the spiritual exercises—prayer, study, service, worship—are you most comfortable with? Which one challenges you the most?

___
___
___

When was the last time you prayed for someone else? Why did you do it, and what happened?

___
___
___

Can you think of a time when you have felt closer to God than you do now? What was happening then, and how did you move away from him?

_____

_____

_____

Chapter 8

Problems are Gifts

When you believe in God and accept Jesus Christ as your Lord and Savior, your life will be perfect; you'll have no more struggles or hardships, and you'll just sail from one happy moment to the next.

Right? Of course not. We're all going to have problems, whether we are believers or not.

We've already discussed this, but it's worth repeating: It's hard to understand why God allows us to have problems and doesn't step in and fix everything. After all, he has the power. He could do that. But it's because he loves us that he doesn't. Instead, he gives us strength and carries us through what we need to do to deal with our problems.

Growth doesn't come without discomfort to some degree—and sometimes it's more than just uncomfortable, it's downright painful. The best way to deal with the distress and hurt that comes with growth is to see the challenges that we experience in life as gifts. Is this another way of offering you a "when life hands you lemons, make lemonade" platitude? No. Sometimes life will hand you lemons and you won't have the sugar, water, and ice it takes to make lemonade. But the lemons are still a gift. It's a cliché, but if every day were beautiful, we wouldn't appreciate it. We need the storms because it takes rain to water the flowers.

> I will lead the blind by a road they do not know, by paths they have not known I will guide them. I will turn the darkness before them into light, the rough places into level ground. These are the things I will do, and I will not forsake them.
>
> Isaiah 42:16 (NRSV)

Okay, enough of the platitudes and clichés. The reality is that when you have problems, it can make you question your faith, but that's okay because questioning your faith can strengthen it.

And remember: When God gives us more than we can handle, it's because he wants us to turn it over to him and let him handle it for us.

God Doesn't Make Mistakes

God is all-powerful and perfect. His judgment is absolutely flawless. So when things happen that you don't understand, don't question God. Accept what has happened and ask God for the wisdom you need to deal with it.

Just as God doesn't make mistakes, he doesn't do things to harm us. When we hurt, he feels our pain. He doesn't enjoy seeing us suffer. So don't blame God when it seems like things aren't going right. Whatever problems you have are not God's fault. In fact, you can save yourself a lot of time and heartache if you don't bother trying to figure out who to blame and simply focus on what to do and how to move forward. Remember, God knows what you need, even when you don't.

> Every word of God is flawless; he is a shield to those who take refuge in him.
>
> Proverbs 30:5 (NIV)

How to Handle Your Problems

There are only two ways to handle a problem: Let God direct you, or try to do it on your own. You're always going to get better results if you do things God's way. He's there to help, and he wants to help—you just have to let him. In fact, very often the source of our problems is that we're trying to control things ourselves instead of relying on God. Certainly in my life when I've been frustrated and not able to get anything accomplished, it's almost always because I was trying to do it myself instead of turning it over to God. I still struggle with this, but I'm getting better at it.

The first step in handling your problems is to pray. Tell God you need his help and ask him what he wants you to do. Then listen. The ability to listen to God is the greatest life skill you can develop.

> "Never bear more than one trouble at a time. Some people bear three kinds—all they have had, all they have now, and all they expect to have."
>
> *Edward Everett Hale*

Remember that God doesn't want us sitting on our hands while we pray, so expect him to direct you to take action of some sort. At the same time, understand that action doesn't always mean motion. Sometimes the action God wants us to take is patient waiting. A lot of people think waiting is doing nothing, but conscious waiting is a form of action.

Once God has told you what to do, do it—and know that you won't be doing it alone. He'll be with you every step of the way.

Looking Back, Looking Forward

We talked about the importance of living in the moment—don't spend time regretting yesterday or worrying about tomorrow. But you should look back long enough to learn from what has happened. Look forward only far enough to know that you have nothing to fear when God is in control of your life, no matter what problems you encounter.

Remember that whatever problems or challenges you experience are only temporary—you are forever!

Please Pray With Me

Loving God,

We know there is no greater love than what you demonstrate for us. We understand that sometimes we will experience problems, challenges, and even pain. We ask that in your love and infinite wisdom, you help us see the good in everything, to understand that problems are gifts and can be used to enrich our lives and the lives of others.

Amen

Your Turn

Think about a problem you have overcome that seemed insurmountable at the time. What did you learn from that experience?

_____
_____
_____

We often use the term "blessing in disguise" to describe something negative that ultimately turned into a positive. When was the last time you experienced a blessing in disguise, and how did you realize it was a blessing?

_____
_____
_____

Chapter 9

Let God Be In Control and Watch What Happens

Your challenge for today, tomorrow, and every day for the rest of your life is to look for the ways that God is working miracles in your life.

Look for the way he talks to you, the way he helps you find direction. God has a hand in every part of your life.

In an interview with ABC's Barbara Walters, convicted Ponzi schemer Bernard Madoff said he was "happier" in prison. According to Walters, Madoff said, "I feel safer here than outside. I have people to talk to, no decisions to

FINDING JOY IN THE MORNING

> Now to him who is able to do immeasurably more than all we ask or imagine, according to his power that is at work within us, to him be glory in the church and in Christ Jesus throughout all generations, for ever and ever! Amen.
>
> *Ephesians 3:20-21 (NIV)*

make. I know I will die in prison. I lived the last 20 years of my life in fear. Now I have no fear because I'm no longer in control."

You don't have to go to prison to feel that way. Turn your life over to God, let him be in control—you will have no fear and you will be freer and more content than you could ever imagine. You will, without a doubt, find joy every morning when God is in control of your life.

Please Pray With Me

Dear God,

Give us victory!

Amen

Part II

How to Find Joy Every Day

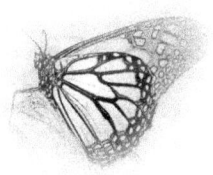

What makes you feel joy?

What can you do to feel that way more often?

Part I of *Finding Joy in the Morning* offered seven strategies for getting through tough times. But we don't have to be going through a crisis to need a little help with getting through the day.

Many of us need help finding joy during normal times—times when things aren't especially tough, but they just aren't as good as they could be. It's possible to live a joyful day, every day. It doesn't take a miracle, it doesn't take a windfall, it just takes doing a few purposeful things every day.

It's easy to get into the habit of giving others control over when we feel joy. And certainly those unexpected bright moments—a compliment from a stranger, a hug from a child, a special simpatico moment with a loved one—are to be treasured. But life is so much richer when we are intentional about joy, when we deliberately

FINDING JOY IN THE MORNING

do things that will bring us joy.

As you read through the suggestions of things you can do to have a joyful day, you may think you don't have time. I get that—we're all busy. But most of these suggestions take no time at all; some take just a few minutes. And when you do them, consciously and deliberately, the results will be more than worth the effort.

You won't have any more hours in the day, but the time that you have will be richer and far more joyful.

So what can you do?

"I used to think that joy was icing on the cake in the Christian life. I no longer think that. Joy is our armor. Joy is what protects us. If we have lost our joy, we have lost everything."

Peter Lowe

Pray

Go to God in prayer every day. Do this not just when you need something, not just when you're on autopilot and chanting a quick prayer while you're thinking of something else, but have a focused, purposeful time of prayer every day.

It doesn't matter where you are or what position you're in. Relax in a chair in your home or go out for a walk. Get on your knees or sit cross-legged in a yoga position. The point is not your posture, the point is prayer. And as you pray, remember to breathe. Take life-giving, deep cleansing breaths that will keep you centered.

There are a number of approaches to prayer that you can use. I regularly use the ACTS and ACTIS method we discussed in Chapter Seven. ACTS stands for adoration, confession, thanksgiving, and supplication. ACTIS adds intercession. Express your adoration for God by praising him; confess your sins (even though he knows about them already); thank God for his wonderful gifts; intercede on behalf of others; and then ask God for the material and spiritual things you want.

Another approach is the five-finger method. Begin with your thumb and pray for those closest to you. Move to your index finger and pray for those that direct you—doctors, pastors, teachers. At your middle finger, pray for those that are "higher ups"—leaders, managers, elected and appointed government officials. At your ring finger, pray for the weakest among us and those in need. Finally, at your pinky finger, pray for yourself.

You can also say the traditional Lord's Prayer. Say it slowly and thoughtfully, considering the meaning behind every word.

> *Our Father, who art in heaven,*
> *Hallowed be thy Name.*
> *Thy Kingdom come.*
> *Thy will be done on earth, as it is in heaven.*
> *Give us this day our daily bread.*
> *And forgive us our debts, as we forgive our debtors.*
> *And lead us not into temptation, but deliver us from evil.*
> *For thine is the Kingdom, and the power, and the glory,*
> *Forever.*
> *Amen.*

However you pray, keep the words from this social media meme in mind: If you are too busy to pray, you are too busy.

Accept that You'll Always Have More Questions Than Answers

When it comes to life in general and God in particular, most of us have a lot of questions. Often getting answers only generates more questions. Accept that you will probably always have more questions than answers. This acceptance will give you peace that will lead to joy.

Our world is full of mysteries. Though we are meant to solve some, we are not meant to solve them all. God wants us to trust him, to have faith that he is in control even when we don't understand what is happening or why.

There's an old saying that when the student is ready, the teacher will appear. When we truly need the answers, God will provide them. And if we are not meant to have the answer, we need to accept that.

This is not an excuse for laziness. Of course, we should seek and study. We're not supposed to stay deliberately ignorant. But when we've given something our best effort and we still don't have the answer, accept it and don't stress over it.

Give Thanks to God

Thank God for all the good things you have and the bad things you don't.

I know it's trite and clichéd, but you can always find something to be thankful for having and something to be thankful for not having—even when it seems like everything is going wrong in your life.

I'm not suggesting that you should ever minimize your troubles. Just because someone has it worse than you doesn't mean you don't have some serious and real problems to deal with. But you still can find some things to be thankful for.

The easiest way to give thanks is to create a gratitude list. Review it and add something to it every day. If you can't think of anything new to add, repeat something. Keep your gratitude list in a notebook, on your computer, or use the *Finding Joy Journal*.

Going through your gratitude list every day delivers two important benefits: One, it causes you to pause and thank God and two, it reminds you of how much you have to be grateful for even when you're dealing with challenges.

While it's important to count your own blessings every day, resist the urge to count the blessings of others. That only leads to envy, and envy will keep you from having a joyful day. Pray for others, but let them be responsible for keeping track of what they're thankful for. Remember, too, that everyone has their own perspective about what's going on in their lives. What is a blessing to one person might not be to someone else. So let others count their own blessings; they know far better than you what those blessings are.

> "Joy is distinctly a Christian word and a Christian thing. It is the reverse of happiness. Happiness is the result of what happens of an agreeable sort. Joy has its springs deep down inside. And that spring never runs dry, no matter what happens. Only Jesus gives that joy. He had joy, singing its music within, even under the shadow of the cross."
>
> *S. D. Gordon*

Say Thank You to Others

As important as it is to thank God, the joy you'll get from expressing gratitude doesn't stop there. Thank other people for what they've done, for the good things they bring to you and the world. Let them know you appreciate what they mean to you and do for you and others.

The first place to start thanking others is at home. Thank your family members for doing chores, running errands, preparing meals, or just making you laugh. Then expand to the people you interact with throughout the day. Thank the receptionist in your office for a warm greeting every morning. Thank the IT folks for keeping your computer working. Thank the store clerk for helping you find what you wanted and getting you checked out promptly. Thank the person who got you the information you needed. Thank the stranger who held a door for you. If you work for a small enough company that you can talk to the owner, thank them for creating the business that created your job. If you work for a larger company, thank your manager or supervisor for everything they do to create a positive, challenging, rewarding workplace.

In addition to thanking people for what they do for you, thank them for what they do for others. Whether you drink coffee or not, thank the person who takes the time to make a fresh pot for the office. Thank the church member who volunteers to help with whatever project is going on. Thank the police officer or firefighter you saw in a store or restaurant for their service.

Do more than say the words—put some meaning behind them. Make eye contact and smile when you speak. And go beyond speaking—write thank-you notes or send a small gift. You don't have to be extravagant, just be mindful of the things people do that deserve thanks and be the one who voices appreciation.

One more thought about giving thanks: As you express your gratitude to others, it's likely that they will begin expressing their gratitude to you. When they do, be gracious. Say, "You're welcome," without denigrating or minimizing what you did. If someone thought enough to thank you, don't say, "Oh, it was nothing." Simply say, "You're welcome."

Give thanks every day, as many times as you can. It costs absolutely nothing to be grateful for what you have, and the joy it will give you is priceless.

Help Someone

Do something to help someone. It can be someone you know or don't know. The point is to be of service.

This doesn't have to be a big, time-consuming effort (although great if you can do that). It could be as simple as carrying a package for someone, picking up something someone dropped, or letting someone go ahead of you in the checkout line so they can get out of the store quickly. If you're going shopping, ask your neighbor if they need anything. If you make a big pot of soup, share part of it with someone who could use a break from cooking. When you bring your trash can in, bring your neighbor's in, too.

When you actively look for ways to be helpful, you'll find that you attract the same behavior from others.

Years ago, I was in the process of moving. I was single at the time and overwhelmed by trying to get everything done without spending a fortune hiring repair people, service providers, and movers. The owner of the small lawn service company I used offered to move me at a cost significantly lower than a traditional moving company would charge. He also did some repairs on my new house, using his knowledge and connections to get the work done for far less than it would have cost from another source.

FIND JOY EVERY DAY

Other friends helped me with the myriad of tasks that go along with buying a house and moving.

A friend of mine was visiting at the time. As she watched me dealing with things, she made the observations, "People just seem to want to help you. It must be that helpless persona you have."

I admit, it still irritates me to remember that, because I don't think I have a helpless persona. To the contrary, I think my persona is confident, independent, and self-sufficient.

But I'm blessed with a family of friends who are kind and generous with their time, knowledge, and resources. I'm blessed to have relationships with service providers who are honest and fair. I believe I am blessed by these people because I try to be a similar blessing to others.

When you make it a point to help someone in some way every day, you'll be blessed by the joy of serving *and* the joy of building rich, rewarding relationships.

"Joy is the serious business of Heaven."

C.S. Lewis

Give Someone the Benefit of the Doubt

To give someone the benefit of the doubt means that you are going to believe them even though you might have some doubt—but no proof—about the truthfulness of what they said. Giving someone the benefit of the doubt means you are choosing to believe something good rather than something bad about the person when you don't have evidence for either case.

Should you always give people the benefit of the doubt? Of course not. In general, you wouldn't give the benefit of the doubt to someone who has a pattern of being untrustworthy. You should also consider how much is at stake. What are you putting at risk by taking the person at their word instead of insisting on proof? I also don't recommend overriding your intuition—if your gut is telling you no, listen to it.

But there are plenty of times when giving someone the benefit of the doubt throws open the doors to let joy in—not only in your life but in theirs as well.

Do Something Good for Your Health

Living a healthy lifestyle can be one of the more challenging things we do. We're busy and surrounded by temptations. Be intentional about doing something every day—even something small—that contributes to your good health.

You don't have to live like or even look like a fitness guru. You don't have to launch a major lifestyle change. And you certainly shouldn't set unrealistic health-related goals. Just do something on purpose that's good for your health.

Some suggestions:
- Exercise—even your regular workout counts.
- Eat something that's good for you.
- Take a vitamin or supplement.
- Decline junk food.
- Take the stairs instead of the elevator.
- Park at the far end of the lot to get the extra walk in.
- Sit up straight.
- Stretch.
- Get a good night's sleep.
- Schedule that medical checkup you've been putting off.
- Floss your teeth.

- Ladies, do a breast self-exam.
- Gentlemen, do a testicular self-exam.

What else can you think of? Do it and make a note of it in your *Finding Joy Journal*.

Let Go of What You Can't Control

Trying to control something that's out of your control is guaranteed to suck all of the joy out of your day. But letting go of what you can't control is far easier said than done for most of us.

Several years ago, a client told me that he put things into two circles—the circle of control and the circle of concern. The circle of control contained things he could do something about; the circle of concern contained things that might affect him but that he couldn't do anything about.

For things in the circle of control, he figured out what he needed to do and took action. For things in the circle of concern, he let go—he didn't worry or even think about them because it was a waste of time and energy. I'm sure he adapted this concept from Stephen Covey's work (Covey's most popular book was *The 7 Habits of Highly Effective People*), and I don't think he was as genuinely nonchalant about the things in his circle of concern as he claimed to be. But the approach is a good one.

If something you can't control is bothering you, let it go. Do it just for today—or maybe even just for a few hours—if that's all you can do. But let it go and see how much room you have for joy in your day.

Change What You Can

When you see something that isn't right, do what you can to change it. You may have to combine this with acceptance because you won't be able to change everything, but your efforts will make a difference.

We're not necessarily talking about monumental results, such as eradicating poverty and disease. Even small changes can add up to big joy. Here's an example: Years ago, several of my neighbors were complaining about the landscaping on the street where the entrance to our community is. When people were turning left both coming into and going out of our neighborhood, they couldn't clearly see the oncoming traffic because of the shrubs. I finally decided to see if anything could be done. I went on the city's website, located the department responsible for the landscaping on that street, and sent an email explaining the problem. The supervisor checked it out and agreed it was a problem. Within a few weeks, the existing landscaping was trimmed back; later, the landscape design was changed to low-height plants. It only took me a few minutes to cause a change that had a positive impact on hundreds of people.

You have more power to be a catalyst for change than you may realize. And who knows? You might just change the world.

Take a Fresh Look

Look at your world as though you'd never seen it before. You'll be surprised at how many things you'll notice that you've been overlooking.

Do this for a few minutes or a few hours. Drive down a street you travel often, looking at the landscape with fresh eyes. Look at your church through the eyes of a first-time visitor (without nitpicking all the little things that need correcting—focus on the good things you've been taking for granted). Take a fresh look at some of the people you deal with regularly—your spouse, family members, friends, and coworkers. Do your job as though it was your first day at the company.

You've heard the old saying that familiarity breeds contempt. I don't think that's true. Familiarity is how we build relationships, establish intimacy, and learn to love. What actually breeds contempt is disrespect and dishonoring others. But sometimes—especially after we've become familiar with them—we take people and things for granted, we're not excited about them anymore. Looking at your world and the people in it through fresh eyes will show you things you've been missing and restore interest and excitement to your day.

> May the God of hope fill you with all joy and peace in believing, so that you may abound in hope by the power of the Holy Spirit.
> *Romans 15:13 (NRSV)*

Make Fun of Yourself

We probably have more funny stories about ourselves than we do about anyone else—after all, we are with ourselves all the time, and we see every silly thing we do. When it's appropriate, share those stories and make fun of yourself.

Some of my stories include:

Looking for my phone when I was talking on it.

The time when I was a young teenager and my gallant boyfriend was trying to help me over a fence (we were taking a neighborhood shortcut) and he dropped me.

The time when I worked for an air freight company and I backed into the wing of an airplane while driving the forklift (I actually have a lot of stories about my abilities as a forklift driver).

Using sugar instead of flour in a recipe (that produced the sweetest cornbread I've ever made).

A humorous, self-depreciating story tells people you don't take yourself in particular or life in general too seriously. It gives them an opening to share something similar. And it makes everyone laugh, one of the easiest ways to add joy to our day.

Spend Time with Your Pet

If you have one (or more), spend some intentional time snuggling with your pet. Talk to it—you can say anything to your pet and be confident it won't be repeated (unless you have a talented parrot). Treasure the unconditional love your pet has for you and let it bring joy to your day.

Enjoy a Special Meal for No Special Reason

It's easy to get into a rut when it comes to eating. In our day-to-day lives, we're always in a hurry and looking for quick and easy things to prepare. We tend to save the special meals—the expensive cuts of meat, the complicated recipes, the nice restaurants—for special occasions like birthdays, anniversaries, and other celebrations.

Either planned or on impulse, celebrate yourself with one of those special meals. And invite someone to join you.

FINDING JOY IN THE MORNING

Care for Your Plants

I have a friend who grows beautiful orchids. She can't understand how I've managed to kill every orchid I've ever had. Though I don't have an abundance of horticulture skill, I do have some plants I've kept alive (one is more than 30 years old and looks like something out of *Little Shop of Horrors*). I like having plants in and around my home—they just need to be low-maintenance with a high tolerance for neglect. Our grandchildren have flower and vegetable gardens—they get to choose what they're going to plant and take great pride in consuming their harvests.

When we care for our plants, we are caring for God's creations, for living things that help clean our air and nourish our bodies. How can you not find joy in that?

"The Lord gives His people perpetual joy when they walk in obedience to Him."
Dwight L. Moody

Exercise

If you've ever watched children in a playground, you know that they move—skipping, running, jumping—for the pure joy of it. They don't need a reason other than the fact that it makes them feel good.

As we get older, it's not unusual to start viewing exercise as just another chore we have to fit into our busy days. And it's often one of the first things we allow ourselves to not do when we don't have enough time. But exercise helps us maintain a healthy body, something scripture tells us is pleasing to God. The Apostle Paul wrote, "Or do you not know that your body is a temple of the Holy Spirit within you, which you have from God, and that you are not your own? For you were bought with a price; therefore glorify God in your body." (1 Corinthians 6:19-20 NRSV)

So get moving, even if it's just for a few minutes. Go for a walk or run. Do a workout. Play a physical game. Get your respiration and heart rate up (safely and only if you are physically able, of course). Let your mind and body regress to childhood and take joy in being in motion.

Take a Social Media Break

For many of us, this one will be hard but step away from social media for a while. Maybe just a few hours, maybe several days.

While the various social media platforms certainly have their benefits, they also have their drawbacks. They often lead us to focus more on what others are doing than on what we should be doing. Because we don't know what our "friends" are using as filters for what they share, many social media platforms present a distorted version of reality and don't allow us to interact with our friends in a substantial and meaningful way.

A break from social media will likely give you a fresh perspective (see Take a Fresh Look), increase your productivity, and strengthen your relationships with your real-world friends.

> But when the Holy Spirit controls our lives he will produce this kind of fruit in us: love, joy, peace, patience, kindness, goodness, faithfulness,
> *Galatians 5:22 (TLB)*

Recite Your Favorite Scripture

If you grew up going to Sunday School and church, you probably spent a lot of time memorizing scripture and can quote a lot of Bible verses. If you didn't—as I didn't—you may find this more challenging, but it's worth it.

There are some good reasons to memorize scripture. Obviously, Jesus memorized Scripture and quoted the Old Testament frequently. Having scripture committed to memory keeps the truth of the Bible fresh in our minds and helps us resist temptation. It helps us share our faith with others.

I have a hard time with the question, "What's your favorite Bible verse?" My answer is, "It depends on what I'm dealing with at the moment."

Take the time—less than a minute!—to say a passage from the Bible that's meaningful to you right now. Do it alone or with others, out loud or to yourself, but do it. Journal it; you may find keeping track of which verses you're quoting will give you valuable insight into how to bring joy to every day.

Learn a New Word

Expand your vocabulary. In addition to the primary definition of a new word, learn the alternate definitions. Look up the origin of the word. Practice pronouncing it. Then look for an opportunity to use it in conversation.

Do an internet search on "word of the day" and you'll see a list of sites that will send you a daily email with a new word.

Find Something Good About Someone You Don't Like

Several years ago I was oversharing some negative comments about a politician on Facebook. A friend of mine who disagreed with me challenged me to say at least one good thing about him. It wasn't easy, but I did it. And while it didn't make me feel particularly joyful, the exercise reminded me that no one is all bad. If you try, you can find something good about anyone.

I still don't like that particular politician, but I've remembered that challenge when dealing with people I don't like on a personal level. If I can't avoid them, I make a concentrated effort to find something good about them and focus on that. Sometimes it merely makes dealing with them tolerable. Other times, it's been the start of a genuine friendship that I would have previously insisted was impossible.

This is one of those things you don't need to do every day (I hope you don't dislike that many people!), but when you encounter someone you don't like, take a moment to find something good about them. Write it in your journal. And see what happens.

> "When our lives are filled with peace, faith and joy, people will want to know what we have."
>
> *David Jeremiah*

Volunteer

Find an organization with a mission you support and volunteer to help. Don't just send money (although that's a good thing to do), get in the trenches and work.

Not all volunteer efforts will produce immediate results or even have a happy outcome. That's not what's important. What's important is to take joy in doing the work.

Let Someone do Something for You

Many of us find that it's far easier to give than to receive. But when we are constantly giving and never receiving, we deny others the joy of giving.

When you let someone do something for you—whether it's as simple as carrying packages to your car or giving you a ride to something more significant such as sitting with you in a hospital or helping you financially—you are allowing them to experience the joy of giving. Take joy in that.

Read Something for Pleasure

Whether it's a book, article, short story or poem, read something for the pure pleasure of it. Don't worry about personal development, self-improvement, or education—find something that you want to read for no reason other than you just want to read it.

We all spend plenty of time reading for school and work. That's a good thing, but not particularly joyful. And too many of us spend way too much time reading social media posts—that doesn't count as reading for pleasure.

Find something you know you'll enjoy and that you don't have a practical reason for reading. Set aside some time, find a comfortable place, and get lost in the words.

Be Deliberately Optimistic

A positive attitude doesn't guarantee a positive outcome, but optimists generally lead more joyful lives than pessimists. Be deliberately optimistic about something—it doesn't matter what, it could be something you are seriously doubtful or absolutely certain about. Choose a situation, look on the bright side, and expect good things to happen.

The worst case scenario is that you'll have to deal with whatever happens—but you won't have allowed yourself to be made miserable by negative anticipation.

Be sure to journal when you do this, so you'll remember the situation and the results. You're likely to find that your optimism will be on target far more often than a pessimistic perspective.

FINDING JOY IN THE MORNING

Say "I Love You"

Do the people you love know that you love them? Probably. Should you tell them anyway? Definitely. Every chance you get.

Expressing your love by what you do is important, but so is saying the words. So say "I love you"—and do it with feeling. None of that automatic "love you, bye now" sort of thing that you say when you're leaving the house or getting off the phone. And don't use it to soften criticism as in, "I love you but ..."

Look the person in the eye and say "I love you" purposefully and intentionally. It will create joy for both of you.

> "Joy is not necessarily the absence of suffering, it is the presence of God."
> *Sam Storms*

Listen

We're all busy. We all have our own opinions. And too many of us are more focused on our electronic devices than we are on the people we're with. So we don't listen.

Schedule time to be with a family member, a friend or just someone who needs a friendly, non-judgmental ear. Step away from your computer. Turn your phone off. Keep your opinions to yourself.

Then listen.

Make eye contact. Confirm that you've heard things correctly. Smile and laugh when appropriate. Ask for more information. Let the person know that nothing is more important to you in that moment than they and what they have to say.

Need some conversation starters? These questions—or variations of them—will help.

- *How was your day?*
- *Tell me about your trip to [wherever you know they've recently been].*
- *What books or movies have you read or seen lately?*
- *How is your [spouse, parent, child or whoever you know is important to them that may be having issues] doing?*
- *How did you and [spouse, partner, long-time friend] meet?*
- *Tell me about your hobby. [Ask for a*

demonstration or for stories about awards or achievements.]

- *How did you get started in your career?*

Listening is one of the greatest gifts you can give yourself and others. Knowing how much joy you're bringing to someone else by genuinely listening to them will bring joy to your day. And who knows what you might learn?

> Dear brothers and sisters, when troubles of any kind come your way, consider it an opportunity for great joy. For you know that when your faith is tested, your endurance has a chance to grow.
>
> *James 1:2-3 (NLT)*

Smile

Make a conscious effort to maintain an attractive expression. You don't have to walk around with a huge grin on your face, but a soft smile and pleasant expression will be reflected back to you from others.

Get Rid of Something You Don't Need

Most of us have too much stuff. Even people who don't have a lot are likely to have things they don't need that are cluttering up their homes, offices, and lives. We know we need to declutter but we don't have time, and the task is too overwhelming.

You don't need to clean out your entire garage or closet or storage area. You don't need to set aside hours or even days to sort, purge, and organize. Just get rid of one thing that you don't need.

Give it to someone, donate it to charity, or simply throw it away. But get rid of it. Then savor the feeling of satisfaction and freedom that comes from letting go of something that didn't need to be taking up space in your world.

Try a New Recipe

One of the things I enjoy about social media is all the interesting recipes that come through my news feed. And I've gotten pretty good at not bothering to save the ones that I know I'll never try. Besides, if I want to make a specific dish, I just Google it, and I'll get hundreds of recipes.

But whether you're cooking for one, two, or a huge family, trying a new recipe can be interesting and entertaining. It's not unusual for me to experiment with a new recipe when we're having guests—although it drives my husband crazy. He likes knowing for sure how the dishes we serve company will turn out. I figure if I've made something inedible we can always call for pizza.

An alternative to trying someone else's recipe is to come up with your own. See what's in the refrigerator and pantry, and create a new signature dish.

Food is essential to life, but it's easy to get into a rut with our meals. Periodically mixing it up (go ahead, eat dessert first) will break up your routine in a way that can bring joy to your day.

Sing

Making music in any form is good for you, but singing is especially beneficial. It's a form of exercise, it improves your posture, it's a natural anti-depressant, and it can lower stress.

If all you do is sing by yourself in the shower or in the car, you'll feel better. Boost the joy singing can bring by joining a church or community choir. If you're really brave, try performing solo.

Singing is something you can do every day to add joy to your world.

> "Joy, not grit, is the hallmark of holy obedience. We need to be light-hearted in what we do to avoid taking ourselves too seriously. It is a cheerful revolt against self and pride."
>
> *Richard J. Foster*

Contact a Friend from Your Past

Reach out to someone you haven't seen or talked with in person in several years. Give them a call or write a note. Suggest getting together. If there's a wound that needs attention, address it. If you just drifted apart because of the demands of your respective lives, acknowledge that.

When you do this, try to be prepared for all possibilities. Your friend may welcome you with open arms and great enthusiasm. Or they may rebuff you without any explanation. Or you may see them and realize that they (or you) have changed, and they are better in your past than your present.

Let the adventure bring you joy.

> You show me the path of life.
> In your presence there is fullness of joy;
> in your right hand are pleasures forevermore.
>
> *Psalm 16:11 (NRSV)*

Be Content

Stop investing all your effort and energy in searching for what you don't have and take the time to see what you do have. This is not to say that you should never strive for more. Goals and aspirations can be good, but they shouldn't cause discontent.

My favorite definition of content is "in a state of peaceful happiness." Most of us don't reach that state passively or by accident; it takes a conscious effort to achieve contentment.

It's okay to want more, but be content with what you have right now.

Laugh

Laugh out loud. It doesn't matter if it's just a chuckle or a giggle, find something that amuses you and express it.

Tell a Joke

If laughing can bring you joy, making someone else laugh is even better. So share a joke. Make it clean, don't rely on humor that comes at someone's expense, and be sure you remember the punch line.

Forgive

Forgiving may be the hardest thing you do, but it will bring you the greatest joy. The reason an Amazon search on "forgiveness" will return hundreds of pages listing books dealing with the topic is because it's important, and we all need help with it.

At the beginning of this section, I said you don't have to do all of the things in this book every day to have a joyful day, but this is one that should be at the top of your daily list. The reason for that is forgiving is rarely a "once and done" thing. If the offense was serious enough to require forgiveness, it's likely that you'll have to forgive more than once.

I can't count the number of times I've forgiven someone and then find myself thinking about what they did and feeling hurt and angry all over again. It's not that I didn't truly forgive them before, it's that forgiveness is a process and sometimes—especially for major hurts but even for smaller slights—we need to do it over and over.

It's important to forgive people even when they're not sorry and they don't want forgiveness. When it comes to forgiving, the wishes of the other person don't matter much. Oh, sure, a family member or friend may ask for forgiveness and may feel better if you say you've forgiven them, but the real beneficiary of forgiveness is the person doing the forgiving.

As you consider who you need to forgive today, remember to forgive yourself. We often find it easier to accept, excuse, and forgive the conduct of others than to do the same with ourselves. Sometimes things that are long in the past come back and haunt me—things I said or did that were hurtful to someone else or just plain dumb. I'll mentally review what happened and try to rewrite the scenes in my head. It never works because I can't do things over, I can't undo a hurt, I can't always make amends—although sometimes I can and that helps tremendously. I just have to forgive myself and move on. When I remind myself that God has forgiven me, it's easier. Note that I said easier, meaning less difficult but still not easy. I have found that if I make the effort to forgive, I can then let the peace of forgiving help me work through the emotions of the situation. Try that and see if it works for you.

Who do you need to forgive today? Stop. Do it. Record it in your journal and feel the joy.

> "If you have no joy, there's a leak in your Christianity somewhere."
>
> *Billy Sunday*

Live in the Moment

When you live in the moment, you can't regret the past or worry about the future—two things that are guaranteed to steal your joy.

Is the moment always perfect and wonderful? No, of course not. Most of the time, the present truly is much better than we realize when we're distracted by worry and regret. But sometimes it's mildly annoying, sometimes it's downright painful. Whatever it is, it's where Jesus wants us to be.

Of course you should plan for the future—that's not the same as worrying. Worry is the brain's way of telling us that we can control something that we can't control. It's a false message. Reject it. When we say the Lord's Prayer, which Jesus taught the disciples to say, we pray, "Give us this day our daily bread." We're not asking for tomorrow's bread. We're not asking for more bread than we need for today so we can save it up. We're asking for our daily bread today and trusting that God will provide tomorrow's bread tomorrow.

Something else to consider: Even if the worst does happen, did it do any good to worry about it beforehand? No. The same approach is good for regrets—you can't undo anything, so accept it and move on. Don't dwell on things you can't change.

Every day, commit to staying in the present. Don't regret yesterday or worry about tomorrow.

Enjoy a Positive Memory

Even as you live in the present, allow yourself a few moments to enjoy a positive memory.

I love remembering moments from the past such as when my husband first told me that he loved me or watching him hold our first grandchild. Or special times from my youth, such as when my (very brave) mother allowed me to drive her car across the old Seven Mile Bridge in the Florida Keys (if you've ever done that, you know why it was so significant) or even all the crazy and silly things my brother did in the name of protecting his little sister.

Taking a brief moment to recall and relive those special times doesn't count as living in the past. It's when those minutes turn into hours and you can't drag yourself into the present that enjoying your memories becomes a problem.

The key to using memories to add joy to your day is to focus only on the positive memories, those moments from the past that will make you smile and feel all warm and fuzzy inside. Go there briefly, find the joy, and bring it back to the present.

Do Something Nice for a Stranger

Think about the times a stranger has done something unexpected that made you feel good. You will feel even better when you're on the giving end.

Do something nice for a stranger, even if it's something as small as holding a door or paying them a compliment—and even if you don't necessarily think they deserve it. If you're thinking something nice in any situation, say it out loud. If the idea of doing something nice crosses your mind, take action on it.

Once when I was putting gas in my car, a man at the pump next to me greeted me and we exchanged some general pleasantries, then he asked if I liked oranges. I said yes and he pulled out a bag of them from his car and gave them to me, saying that his trees had produced a bumper crop and he didn't want them to go to waste. Now, I confess that I was reluctant to consume fresh fruit handed to me by a total stranger (who knows if he was genuinely the nice guy he seemed to be or if the oranges were tainted in some way?), but the experience brightened my day and still makes me smile.

Need some ideas of things you can do? Try these:

- *Let someone go ahead of you in the checkout line.*
- *Let a car get in front of you in traffic (even if the driver has been rude).*
- *Tell a frazzled parent that their child is cute, sweet and well-behaved (even if it's not entirely true).*
- *Offer to take the grocery cart back to the store from the parking lot for someone.*
- *Tell someone you like the slogan on their T-shirt.*
- *Pick up the check for the person in line behind you at the coffee shop.*
- *If you see someone struggling with anything—carrying packages, loading a car, wrangling kids or pets—offer to help.*

Make eye contact and smile when you do it so they know you are being intentional.

> "You can't live a perfect day until you do something for someone who will never be able to repay you."
>
> *John Wooden*

Affirm Your Worth

You are a child of God, you are one of God's creations, and you have value.

Remind yourself of this every day. Write it in your journal. Look in the mirror and say it out loud.

Your value is not in what you provide for others, it's in who God made you. It's not superficial—God doesn't waste his time on things that aren't important and he made you, so you're important.

One caveat to this joy exercise: If you have low self-esteem or a distorted sense of value driven by abuse in your past, you may need professional help to deal with those issues. I know from personal experience that those scars run deep and can't be healed with simple affirmations. But sometimes even the most well-adjusted of us need to be reminded of our worth—why not do it every morning to get your day off on the right foot?

Learn Something New

Even if it's something small, learn something new. Exercise your mind and enjoy the sense of achievement you get.

Be Awed by the Beauty of our World

Our world isn't perfect. But in spite of the fact that it has plenty of ugliness and evil, it's still beautiful in big and small ways. Unfortunately, we're often too preoccupied to notice.

Take a moment to be awed by the beauty of our world. This may not be easy if you are in a place (either figuratively or literally) without much beauty, but if you focus, you can do it. Then write about it in your journal so you can remind yourself of it when you need to.

> "The smallest act of kindness is worth more than the greatest intention."
>
> *Kahlil Gibran*

Study God's Word

Read the Bible every day—even if it's just one verse. When we fill our mind with God's Word, He will fill our hearts with joy.

Going beyond simply reading the Bible to actually studying it is another way to find joy. In addition to reading the Bible and trying to comprehend it, read other books and articles that will help your understanding of this amazing book.

Yes, I know that the works of many Biblical scholars are dry and almost as difficult to understand as many parts of the Bible. Look for resources that are geared to the busy layperson—people who are not necessarily interested in preaching or teaching to large audiences, but who want to grow in their faith and knowledge of God's Word.

You could also read an uplifting devotion or article by authors you know and trust. Find short essays that will touch your heart, make you smile or cry, and give you insight into God's infinite wisdom and desires for his children.

> "Joy is strength."
> *Mother Teresa*

Say Something Positive

Every time you think something positive about someone, say it out loud. Don't assume they know or that they'll think you're strange, tell them.

Be generous—but honest!—with compliments. If the best you can do is something superficial, such as to compliment someone on their appearance, that's fine. But if you can, go deeper. And be specific. Don't just say, "You're so thoughtful." Instead, cite a particular incident of the other person's thoughtfulness in action.

Tell people that you appreciate them. It's one of the simplest things you can do and has an incredibly powerful impact on the person you're talking to.

The idea is to regularly say things that magnify others' strengths, not their weaknesses.

You'll do more than brighten someone's day—you could potentially change their life for the better. And that will certainly bring joy to your day.

Eliminate Negative Self-Talk

One of my favorite social media memes is a picture my husband took of a gorilla; the text reads, "Don't put yourself down. That's no way to talk about God's creation."

God made us in his image. When we say negative things about ourselves, we are saying negative things about God. God can handle it, but it's not good for us.

Negative self-talk—those unpleasant and destructive thoughts that run through our minds and sometimes make their way to our lips—can be insidious because we often don't realize we're doing it. But it can sap the joy out of our days.

There are plenty of ways to eliminate negative self-talk—a Google search on "how to eliminate negative self-talk" will produce millions of results with all kinds of advice and techniques for turning off those nasty little voices in your head. What it all comes down to is this: If you wouldn't say it to someone you love, don't say it to yourself.

Tell God that You Trust Him

Tell God that you trust him.

Yes, he knows it, but tell him—and do it every day. Say, "I trust you, God. I know that you will guide me, protect me, comfort me and give me the strength I need to live out your will for my life."

It's a commitment you're making as much to yourself as you are to him.

It's fine to say that we trust in God. It's far more powerful to personally tell God specifically that you trust him. Do it every day—and follow through on your commitment.

> "Happiness is untested delight. Joy is delight tested."
>
> *Jack Hylesr*

Closing Thoughts

I wish just reading this book would assure you a joyful life from this time forward. The reality is that living a joyful life is not something you can figure out and be done with it. It's something you have to work on every day.

You don't have to do all of the things suggested in this book every day, but the more of them you do, the more joyful your days will be. And here's a wonderful bonus: Adding joy to your own life is like throwing a pebble into a pond. Your joy creates ripples of joy for others that will spread far and wide.

Use a journal to keep track of what you do. Jot things down during the day, then review them before you go to bed. Some of the more challenging things, such as forgiving and letting go of what you can't control, may become easier after you journal and see the pattern of how much better you feel when you do them. And if you want to give your day a kick start, review yesterday's entries first thing each morning.

Life is an unassembled gift. It becomes what you make it, so make it joyful.

Index to Part II

Pray	129
Accept that You'll Always Have More Questions Than Answers	131
Give Thanks to God	132
Say Thank You to Others	134
Help Someone	136
Give Someone the Benefit of the Doubt	138
Do Something Good for Your Health	139
Let Go of What You Can't Control	140
Change What You Can	141
Take a Fresh Look	142
Make Fun of Yourself	144
Spend Time with Your Pet	145
Enjoy a Special Meal for No Special Reason	145
Care for Your Plants	146
Exercise	147
Take a Social Media Break	148
Recite Your Favorite Scripture	149
Learn a New Word	150
Find Something Good About Someone You Don't Like	150
Volunteer	151
Let Someone do Something for You	152

FINDING JOY IN THE MORNING

Read Something for Pleasure	152
Be Deliberately Optimistic	153
Say "I Love You"	154
Listen	155
Smile	157
Get Rid of Something You Don't Need	157
Try a New Recipe	158
Sing	159
Contact a Friend from Your Past	160
Be Content	161
Laugh	161
Tell a Joke	161
Forgive	162
Live in the Moment	164
Enjoy a Positive Memory	165
Do Something Nice for a Stranger	166
Affirm Your Worth	168
Learn Something New	169
Be Awed by the Beauty of our World	169
tudy God's Word	170
Say Something Positive	171
Eliminate Negative Self-Talk	172
Tell God that You Trust Him	173

Would you like to use *Finding Joy in the Morning* for a group study?

Download a free copy of the Leader's Guide and receive a discount code for bulk purchases of the print version. Go to:

CreateTeachInspire.com/leader

Finding Joy Journal

Keep a journal of what gives you joy. Any kind of a notebook—either paper or digital—will work for your journal. If you need a little more structure, check out the *Finding Joy Journal*.

Use the *Finding Joy Journal* to keep track of what brings you joy, let go of what doesn't, and guide you along your own joyful journey.

**Order your copy now at
CreateTeachInspire.com/journal**

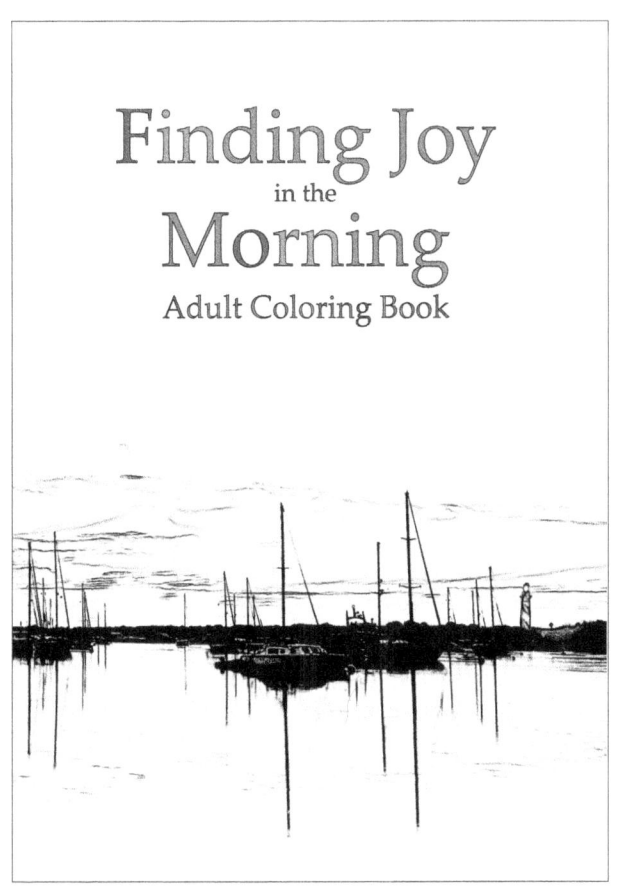

Color the words and pictures that bring you joy!

Order your copy at

CreateTeachInspire.com/color-joy

Bonus!

Words to Work By

Thank you for reading *Finding Joy in the Morning*. Please accept the following three devotions from *Words to Work By: 31 devotions for the workplace based on the Book of Proverbs* as an expression of my gratitude.

Jacquelyn Lynn

1
Value

Such is the end of all who go after ill-gotten gain; it takes away the lives of those who get it.

Proverbs 1:19

Are you stealing from your employer? How about from your customers?

The term workplace theft is usually used to describe embezzling money or taking equipment or supplies without permission. But there's another way theft occurs in the business world: When individuals fail to deliver the full value pledged in exchange for the agreed-on compensation.

We tend to think of wages in terms of what the employer pays rather than what the employee provides in exchange for the money. Similarly, we tend to think of products in terms of cost (price) rather than value (worth).

Whether you are an individual selling your labor as an employee, a service provider being paid as an independent contractor, or a business selling a product, at a very minimum you should provide what you promised in exchange for the compensation you receive. To do anything less is to steal from those who are paying you. To do more is a demonstration of your own integrity.

When you steal from others, you rob yourself. When you give less than your best, you erode your sense of self-worth. When you fail to respect and meet your own obligations, you diminish your ultimate value.

But when you refuse to steal, you enrich yourself. When you give your absolute best, you can be confident in your value. When you meet your commitments, you know you have performed with honor.

Those are the gains worth having in life. They create the life God wants us to live.

BONUS

Dear God,

Please give me the strength and wisdom to consistently do Your will and my best, to exceed expectations in all my transactions and relationships.

Amen

2

Understanding

Discretion will protect you, and understanding will guard you.

Proverbs 2:11

A man with three young children boarded a commuter train, took a seat, bowed his head and covered his eyes. The kids sat quietly for a few moments, then started moving around. It wasn't long before they were running up and down the aisle, laughing and screaming at each other, bumping into other passengers. All the while, their father sat still, apparently ignoring them.

Finally a passenger spoke up. "Excuse me, sir," he said, annoyance obvious in his voice. "Please get your children under control. They're making it impossible for the rest of us to ride in peace."

The man raised his head and stared bleakly at the passenger who had spoken aloud what everyone else on the train was thinking. "I'm sorry," he said. "We just left the hospital where their mother died. I don't know how to tell them and I don't know what to do."

Variations on this story have been circulating for years. It may or may not be true, but the message is important: Before you make a judgment or take action on something involving others, try to understand what's going on in the other person's life that is not immediately evident.

Whether you are a coworker or a supervisor, be slow to criticize or condemn a change in behavior, attitude or performance. External behavior is often just a symptom of more serious underlying circumstances – circumstances that might need anything from just a little time and understanding to some major assistance to work out.

Of course, you have a job to do and a business to run – which is all the more reason for you to seek to understand what is not readily apparent and determine an appropriate course of action. It's good business to do what you can to retain experienced workers, even if it means helping them through a personal rough patch. Whatever you do, be discreet and keep confidences. Repeat nothing without explicit permission. Be someone people can trust to see their side, offer appropriate assistance and protect their privacy.

BONUS

Dear God,

When someone is having a problem, give me the ability to look below the surface, to see beyond the symptoms to the cause, to understand how to help, and to do it all with the utmost of discretion.

> Amen

3

Reward

Do not withhold good from those who deserve it, when it is in your power to act.

Proverbs 3:27

Research tells us that a primary reason people steal from their employers is because they feel they aren't being adequately compensated through their wages. They don't think they're doing anything wrong because they see what they've stolen as something they're entitled to. Research also tells us that while money is important to workers, it's not the only thing – and often not the top thing – that motivates them.

Years ago, I worked with a supervisor who never uttered a word of thanks or praise to his team. Once I mentioned that one of the junior people could use a few words of appreciation and encouragement, and he said, "He gets his 'appreciation' in his paycheck every week. That's thanks enough." Not long after that, the young man who was only thanked by getting paid accepted a job offer from a competing company – and he took several valuable customers with him. While he was doing essentially the same work, his new employer offered a more prestigious title, a slightly higher wage, advancement opportunities, and recognition for a job well done.

Regardless of where you are in the corporate hierarchy – and indeed in all aspects of your life – don't be stingy with recognition and commendation. Whether you are the janitor or the CEO, when people around you deserve an expression of appreciation or praise, give it to them. It takes just a few seconds to say, "Good job," or to send an email or IM that says, "Thanks for what you did."

Don't limit your thanks and praise to colleagues and subordinates – the president of the company can use a little positive reinforcement every now and then, too!

If you control wages, be as generous as possible with base salary, bonuses and benefits while still being fiscally responsible. From a very practical perspective, you'll see less turnover and greater loyalty on your staff. Even more important is that you'll be running your operation the way God wants you to.

BONUS

Dear God,

Keep me alert to opportunities to be generous with those I work with. Help me notice the good they do and recognize it with my own words and deeds.

                                                    Amen

Jacquelyn Lynn finds joy in her faith, family, and friends, and in the knowledge that she is living God's purpose for her life. She is a Presbyterian elder and deacon and the author of more than 30 books. She is also the co-creator of a series of Christian coloring books for adults.

For more information or to contact her:
CreateTeachInspire.com

Our faith is a part of who we are.
We don't leave it at the door when we go to work.

But sometimes in the mad chaos of today's business world, we need the peace, comfort and guidance that a brief devotion and prayer can bring.

Words to Work By: 31 devotions for the workplace based on the Book of Proverbs by Jacquelyn Lynn is a collection of inspiration and motivational thoughts taken from the teachings of the world's greatest business advisor: King Solomon.

In *Words to Work By*, you'll find:

• Short, to-the-point devotions that are ideal to begin your work day, open a meeting or just take a break

• Prayers that offer gratitude and petitions for the business/work side of our lives

• True stories to provide real-life guidance that is as applicable today as it was thousands of years ago

• Appropriate messages and motivation for any worker, from entry-level to senior executive and entrepreneurs

God's Word was, is and always will be appropriate and relevant—for life and for business.

Available in paperback or Kindle version.

Visit **WordsToWorkBy.com** to get your copy of ***Words to Work By*** today.

www.ingramcontent.com/pod-product-compliance
Lightning Source LLC
Chambersburg PA
CBHW071731080526
44588CB00013B/1985